SELF-LOVE HANDBOOK Magnified with Law of Attraction

***

Instantly Shift into Self-Love, Heal Your Life & Create the Abundance of Joy You Deserve

By Elena G. Rivers

Copyright Elena G. Rivers © 2019

www.LOAforSuccess.com

All rights reserved. No part of this publication may be reproduced, stored in a retrieval system, or transmitted, in any form or by any means, electronic, mechanical, photocopying, recording or otherwise, without the prior written permission of the author and the publishers.

The scanning, uploading, and distribution of this book via the Internet or via any other means without the permission of the author is illegal and punishable by law. Please purchase only authorized electronic editions, and do not participate in or encourage electronic piracy of copyrighted materials.

Elena G. Rivers © Copyright 2019 - All rights reserved.

Legal Notice:

This book is copyright protected. It for personal use only.

Disclaimer Notice:

Please note the information contained in this document is for educational and entertainment purposes only. Every attempt has been made to provide accurate, up to date and completely reliable information. No warranties of any kind are expressed or implied.

Readers acknowledge that the author is not engaging in the rendering of legal, financial, medical or professional advice. By reading this document, the reader agrees that under no circumstances are we responsible for any losses, direct or indirect, which are incurred as a result of the use of information contained within this document, including, but not limited to, errors, omissions, or inaccuracies.

The information presented in this publication is not designed to replace any professional therapy or medical advice from a qualified health provider. If you suffer from any medical conditions, are depressed or on medication, be sure to consult with a professional.

The content of this book is designed as a simple, uplifting, self-help book to help you improve your motivation and create healthy lifestyle habits.

Introduction- Why Self-Love is the Only Way to Create the Life You Love and That Loves You Back .. 6

Chapter 1 Step #1 Emotional Peeling 26

Chapter 2 Step #2 Making Friends with Your Emotions.. 42

Chapter 3 Step #3 Control Your Precious Mind 50

Chapter 4 Step #4 The Number One Self-Love Trick to Eliminate Limiting Beliefs and Self-Doubt 60

Chapter 5 Step #5 Expressing Kindness 71

Chapter 6 Step #6 Creative Self Expression 75

Chapter 7 Step #7 Positive Reminders and Your Own Magic Pendulum.. 79

Chapter 8 #Step 8 Magnifying LOA: Combine Action with Attraction.. 82

Super Addictive Self-Love, Self-Care, Self-healing and Self-Wellness Recipes from Elena 86

A Special Offer from Elena to Help You Manifest Faster 109

More Books written by Elena G.Rivers................... 110

Introduction- Why Self-Love is the Only Way to Create the Life You Love and That Loves You Back

Are you ready to experience more love and light in your life?

Do you want to transform negative into positive?

Do you want to embrace the true, authentic you and let opportunities come to you? How about attracting people who care about you and want your highest good?

And what if you could almost instantly shift into self-love, magnify it with the Law of Attraction and totally transform your energy?

My intention behind writing this book is to help you unleash the true, divine you while enhancing your intuition and aligning yourself with the universal wisdom so that you can receive unlimited guidance on your journey.

While many people may mistakenly reject self-love as some kind of a buzzword, or an unnecessary ritual, we both know that you are here for a reason. You know that the answers you have been searching for are there for you, and the only gate you need to allow yourself to open is the gate of self-love.

I am here to guide you through the process that helped me on my journey and to offer you an invitation to become the master of your emotions, heart, mind and soul.

Many people mistake self-love for self-interest, manipulation or even ego driven actions.

However, self-interest and ego driven actions are not the same as self-love.

INTRODUCTION - WHY SELF-LOVE IS THE ONLY WAY

Self-love is about stepping into your divine light so that you can inspire those around you.

Self-love is the foundation that will help you experience higher vibrations, unforgettable experiences and a true abundance in all areas of your life so that you feel fulfilled.

Self-love is the gate to your inner leadership. That divine, magnetic light that you are now giving yourself the permission to shine.

That light has the power to polarize your life in a very authentic way. You will feel empowered to say *no* to people, circumstances and events that no longer serve you.

People who try to manipulate you or to take advantage of you will not only lose their power, but they will also learn the negative consequences of their actions, which eventually will help them transform too. People who behave in ways that are designed to cause pain to, or take advantage of, other human beings very often operate from a place of self-loathing and are doing what they have been programmed to do.

Focusing on the negative, or turning down to those hurting, detrimental levels of self-hate is not the answer.

Love and self-love are the answer. Stepping up and stepping away at the same time is the answer.

Becoming your own leader first, so that you can then become a meaningful, heart driven leader to those around you. Whether it's for your family, friends, local community, a company you work for or your clients.

In my case it's my beloved readers.

This book is a passion project of mine and the lessons I am sharing are the lessons I acquired on my own journey of self-discovery, while learning about the Law of Attraction and holistic self-development.

INTRODUCTION - WHY SELF-LOVE IS THE ONLY WAY

The journey consists of patterns that I knew existed but even though I attempted writing this book many times, I found it very hard to express myself in a way that others could easily understand and follow.

At first, I thought the answer was in taking more writing classes so that I could become a better writer.

I thought, *I probably have the writer's block. It will go away as soon as I learn a few "hacks"*.

Yet I still felt very blocked. Finally, I decided to do an experiment, and focus entirely on self-love. I committed myself to getting rid of the resistance. I focused on letting go of the outcome and just doing exactly what I am sharing in this book, all over again. That helped me improve and internalize the process I am now fully ready to teach. As a bonus, it also aligned me into my intuition and to the Universe.

Now as I am working on the pages of this book, the process is very enjoyable and almost effortless. I can feel a nice twinging sensation in my head as well as in my heart and hands. It feels as if God, the Universe and the Divine part of me and you communicate with me and share the message that it is my mission to put down on paper.

That experience has helped me release the last "drops" of resistance and has given me clarity and empowerment.

I learned to forgive myself and step into unlimited self-love.

This is the self-love that I live and breathe. This is the self-love that is my lifestyle, and my purpose. This is the self-love that I commit to full-time, not part time.

Through that enlightening commitment, I am now able to share this gift with you, and I am forever grateful for the opportunity.

I totally understand that most people may be challenged with the idea of "self-love". I can totally understand that, because I have been there too.

INTRODUCTION - WHY SELF-LOVE IS THE ONLY WAY

For years, I damaged my wellbeing with unhealthy habits and artificial masks, while stepping away from my talents and authenticity.

That negative pattern started when I was in high school where the English teacher used to laugh at my "funny" accent and at the grammatical errors in my writing.

Coming from a family of poor immigrants and living in a foreign country, I felt excluded and worthless. I remember that I only had one friend who wanted to hang out with me, but very soon, other kids convinced her to leave me. While everyone was getting ready for her birthday party, I was excluded. Someone even said, "The party is only for those who will bring some birthday gifts and Elena is too poor for that anyways so it's better if she stays at home."

If I'd had the self-love and empowerment, I carry in my heart right now, I would have respected myself enough to immediately say, "Don't react Elena, these are just triggers. People who say those hurtful words need self-love too." I would not now react (or over-react) as I used to.

But back then, I had no idea about self-love, the law of attraction or spiritual self-help.

It was back then that the feeling of being completely excluded and not feeing worthy led me to destructive habits and behaviors. Like, for example, going on sugar spree. I would stuff myself with all kinds of bagels and ice cream. I wanted to go back home, watch TV, and eat all that food.

In my late teenage years, I found a new group of "friends" who wanted to hang out with me, and they were all from a similar, poor immigrant background. We all shared the same fears and experiences. Unfortunately, that group got me into destructive habits of drinking, smoking and using other substances.

I had some illusional moments of belonging and feeling loved and enjoying the company of "friends".

INTRODUCTION - WHY SELF-LOVE IS THE ONLY WAY

However, I soon learned that they all laughed at me behind my back and just wanted to use me. I tried so hard to be like them, wear similar clothes, skip school and just be cool like them, so that they would love me and accept me.

Then I repeated the same pattern all over again throughout my twenties and thirties. Both in my personal life and in careers I had.

I would never listen to myself, I would never love myself and I would never approve of myself. Instead, I felt unworthy and wanted others to approve of me first. I had to experience the same pattern dozens of times until something clicked in me. I knew I had to shift my energy from being a victim to being someone who is empowered so that other people can feel this energy too.

You know what they say about people who fear dogs? The dogs can sense that fear and this may lead them to attack the person who fears them. And so, the vicious cycle carries on.

The same happens when a person is not feeling worthy and cuts themselves off from self-love. That vibration attracts people who also feel that way and their way of feeling better is, very often, to use, manipulate and hurt other people.

The best way to avoid such toxicity in your life is to shift to self-love which will help you elevate your energy, feelings and actions.

Many people I had the pleasure to teach my self-love process to came to a simple conclusion: "Oh my God, the goals I was chasing for so many years were not really my own. I never cared about that career, job, client or business. For years I was wondering why I couldn't manifest this or that. Now I understand that what I wanted to manifest wasn't even for me. Instead, I have always wanted to..."

Those "aha something clicked" moments are amazing. People are waking up to their true divine selves where they step into their passion and purpose while leaving self-judgment and judgment from other people. That completely erases self-doubt and helps align with meaningful inspired action.

INTRODUCTION - WHY SELF-LOVE IS THE ONLY WAY

There is no more pushing and fighting.

There is only empowerment. You wake up, you know your *why*, you know what to do and you do it while really loving the process. Your energy levels are much higher, because you no longer need to go against the flow. Instead you go with it and you love who you're becoming.

I now love myself. I now treat myself with care.

This is true self love. It's not self-interest. Real self-love helps you unleash your full potential and gives you the courage to share it with other people. That gives you even more strength and motivation.

This book is designed to be read more than once. That's because each time you read it, you will go through a new shift while getting on a higher and higher vibration. You can also use it on a bad day. Just read a few random pages to help you shift. I also warmly invite you to have a clear intention behind reading this book. Perhaps you are thinking, "Will it work for me? Isn't it just another self-help book? Will I be able to transform?"

Let me get this straight. This is not about me and this book.

I don't write to be famous.

I do it to share my message.

Focus on yourself and your intention. The suggested intention for you should be, "Self-love will change me and my life."

Trust the process. Some things may take longer. The journey never stops; therefore, it should be as enjoyable as possible.

Also, this is not just another "self-improvement book."

While there are many amazing books in that category, I am not a big fan of the term "self-improvement" because it implies that we are not good enough and that we need to improve by constantly looking outside of ourselves.

INTRODUCTION -WHY SELF-LOVE IS THE ONLY WAY

However, the right self-love mindset should be this:

I am open to learning and grateful for people who provide books and materials to feed my mind with positive information and empowerment.

I am already enough. I am already good enough. I am already worthy.

All the answers are within me, I love diving deep to find them.

Reading helps me reconnect to the deep wisdom within me.

It's a real game changer and a great intro into self-love.

As I have mentioned, throughout my childhood and teenage years as well as my twenties and thirties I struggled with self judgement and very low self-esteem. I was chasing other people's goals and status and moving away from my light in order to get approved by other people. I was creating my own trap and constantly feeling pain. Eventually I got used to it. But deep inside I knew that there was some meaning to it.

I knew that eventually I could turn that pain into some kind of lessons or activities that could help other people. While most people never admit their pain, trauma and suffering (and it's not their fault because we have all been conditioned to wear masks), deep inside they know they need to heal. They understand that they deserve to access the healing power of self-love to transform and help their loved ones transform too.

During those years of suffering, I was still searching for that one thing that could help me. At first, I thought it was motivation, or productivity. I thought, *I could achieve more and be more successful. Then, people will look up to me.* And yes, back then I did have a couple of successful businesses, but those businesses eventually led me into a burnout.

INTRODUCTION -WHY SELF-LOVE IS THE ONLY WAY

At one point I was so sick that I could not work. I had to let go of my business to focus on my health. And then, again, most "friends" left me.

Don't get me wrong. Motivation and productivity are great. It's good to learn different ways to stay motivated and to organize our activities in a productive way.

But...without self-love, both motivation and productivity can be traps. You can motivate yourself with inspirational speeches, affirmations and you can drink lots of coffee to "keep going" or "get the stuff done."

Superficial success like that doesn't make you happy. It can temporarily motivate you. But it's like building a house on sand. When it goes down it goes down. And it will go down quickly.

At the same time, motivation and productivity do make a difference if you take action that you really want to take. An action that aligns with your ultimate vision that is approved by the Divine You.

You pursue a goal, career or business that you are really passionate about and that you want to pursue. Or one that you think is good for you and you don't care about what other people think.

That's self-love. And from that place- it makes total sense to learn motivational and productivity techniques.

Before my transformation, I tried everything to ease the pain.

Aside from using destructive habits to quickly feel better, I also started researching self-development. I knew I could find my long-term answers in that field.

At some point, I thought I needed more confidence. As a result, I hired a success coach and a confidence coach. I learned many useful techniques. I am sure those coaches had amazing intentions. Unfortunately learning more about confidence did not go to the root of the problem, which was a lack of self-love.

INTRODUCTION - WHY SELF-LOVE IS THE ONLY WAY

Instead, I learned to wear superficial masks and speak with authority, so that when I had clients on the phone, I could get more sales. But I did not enjoy working with many of those clients. Often, we were not a good match anyway. So, the business wasn't going anywhere, even though I used to hit all my revenue goals every month.

I had what most entrepreneurs call "predictable income". Leads and clients. I knew that a certain number of calls would translate into a certain number of clients and money made in the front end. I also knew how many of those clients would stay with us and add more revenue to the backend of my old business.

Unfortunately, I was acting out of alignment.

Don't get me wrong, we were doing a great service. The clients were happy. But I was unfulfilled and burned out.

The money I made very often disappeared quickly because I was drinking as well as overspending on clothes and items I didn't need.

Okay, I just need to book another holiday. I need to post pictures from expensive hotels on social media. People will like that and comment on it. Then I will feel worthy and deserving, then I will love myself.

Oh...and if my old high school friends who did not want to hang out with me and my old teachers see how well I am doing, and how well I live, and how much money I make, then they will accept me. Then I will be able to love myself and feel at peace.

I could never relax on those holidays. I would look at my phone, my agenda and my laptop all the time. I was too afraid to lose my business to take a break.

At some point I hoped that would change when I hired an assistant. *Then I can relax, and she will take care of those phone calls,* I thought.

INTRODUCTION - WHY SELF-LOVE IS THE ONLY WAY

Okay, so I hired an assistant and it all went well. At first, I gained a bit more free time. But, as always, negative patterns sneaked in again. I would either indulge in workaholism, thinking, *Okay, now that my assistant takes care of some admin tasks, I can focus more on strategy and learning.* I would take on more clients and more business just to feel worthy, and just to show I was okay, I was successful, and I was something.

During that time many bad things happened to me. I even attracted a greedy and unethical accountant who saw that I was easy prey and managed to "legally steal" some of my money.

The same patterns manifested through unethical business associates, or clients who were a real pain in the neck. And, no matter how hard I worked, the money would always leave me. It was just spinning around.

I would constantly be on a spiral of self-destructive behaviors. Extensive partying, extreme workaholism or overspending on items and travels to relax. But I could never relax. Many of those travels would only make me drink more because I felt so scared to go back to the hell I had created for myself.

Heck, even when I learned about the Law of Attraction, at first I did not use it properly. I didn't have enough courage to go deep, to get rid of the old, negative patterns and destructive emotional layers that were driving my own behaviors.

At first, when I got into LOA, I would operate from a place of self-doubt and not being enough and I would magnify the bad.

I don't mean to be judgmental, but in a so-called spiritual community, you can find two kinds of leaders. Some leaders are really passion driven and their offerings are always based on the highest value and good to help people transform. Those leaders were the ones who helped me on my journey and got me onto the path of self-enlightenment. Unfortunately, there are also some individuals who, whether on purpose or unconsciously, create offerings that are

INTRODUCTION - WHY SELF-LOVE IS THE ONLY WAY

designed to make people spin their wheels. The second group of leaders- well...they still need to heal. They still need self-love.

Luckily, when you step into unlimited self-love, you will be able to attract the guidance of good people who already love themselves and who love you too. People who understand the concept of "only for the highest good of the Whole." Your intuition will be enhanced to such a level that you will feel whether something is off or not. So, you will not feel like signing up for a seminar or a program if you feel that the energy of the people offering it is not the right energy for you.

You will be able to walk away from things that no longer serve you with a simple, non-judgmental approach. What does not help you may still help someone else who is still on a different journey and that is totally fine.

That is why, through this book, we will take a holistic approach. We will help you heal from the inside out. Some uncomfortable truths may come to the surface. You may even feel like crying but these are normal experiences on a path of self-healing.

Please note that you can reach out to me via email should you have any questions about this book.

The best way to do so is to join my Newsletter and reply to the first email I send you. (I handle those emails personally. They don't go to my assistant.)

Visit:

www.LOAforSuccess.com/newsletter

so that we can stay in touch and you can keep inspired.

INTRODUCTION - WHY SELF-LOVE IS THE ONLY WAY

Also please note that this book is not intended as a substitute for professional therapy with a qualified mental health professional. Throughout this book I only share my experiences and the step-by-step process that helped me and I am always happy to answer readers' questions in private. However, in some cases you may want to speak to a professional therapist which is totally fine. If needed, give yourself the permission to do that, because it's also an act of self-love and being okay with sometimes not being okay and seeking expert guidance you need to make the next sacred step on your journey to inner peace.

Now, back to this handbook...Start with that commitment. Love and approve of yourself now.

Become aware of those voices in your head. Don't judge them as that is judging the fact that you have been judging yourself.

That voice that tells you that you are not worthy. That voice that says you are not good enough. These are voices that are not really yours. They come from social conditioning.

We need more magnetic, self-love warriors to help transform the world.

Pay attention to your thoughts. Are they in or out of alignment with yourself? Remember you can dismiss all the thoughts. You can easily let them go. They don't mean anything. You can put them into a balloon and release them.

Because you are lovable, you love and approve of yourself. Someone out there in the world is now waiting for you, another self-love warrior.

The side effect of self-love is unstoppable motivation. There will be much less self-doubt and eventually you will be able to powerfully erase it.

The process contained in this healing handbook will help you re-wire your brain. You will feel fully present, almost euphoric. Every moment will be magical. People will be curious to learn from you,

INTRODUCTION -WHY SELF-LOVE IS THE ONLY WAY

they will be naturally attracted to you. And, at the same time, critics will melt away, as your light will be too much for some and the light will keep you safe.

Consciously choose to embody the here and now. You will shine more and more every moment. Whether you are working, driving, shopping or relaxing, every moment will be magical like it was meant to be.

You will realize when and how you're acting out of alignment and that will easily allow you to get rid of old habits.

Your sense of intuition will be enhanced, you will instantly know the answer to the question: "Does it feel light or heavy?"

You will know what you need to let go of and as you get rid of those emotional layers it will really feel amazing.

You will be naturally motivated to get hooked on healthy activities like meditation instead of browsing through your Facebook feed.

The way you interpret certain events or circumstances will change. For example, if, on some nights you will not be able to fall asleep, instead of stressing out about it, you will see it as a sign. "It means I need to meditate or do yoga or have a relaxing essential oil bath." As a result of that, you will never struggle with insomnia or anxiety again. You will know how to nip it in the bud and stop overacting once and for all. You will no longer feel jealous or feel as if others have or do this and that and you need to take their path too.

Because of your light, and being in full alignment with your purpose, you will get connected to your true gifts that the world needs. That will allow you to be of service while following your passion in such a way that you will find yourself attracting career opportunities you enjoy, doing work that is meaningful and, if that is your goal, leads to fame or appreciation.

You will know which path will make you happy because your extra sense of perception will be enhanced.

INTRODUCTION - WHY SELF-LOVE IS THE ONLY WAY

Self-love is one of the most rewarding gifts you can offer yourself. Acting in a way you love and enjoy that is in the highest interest of all.

Perhaps you have some passion project you have been postponing? Maybe you want to change your job or attract your dream clients into your business? After reading this book, you will feel fully recharged and inspired to pursue your passion. If you don't know what your passion is, don't worry at all. The process outlined in this handbook will help you re-wire your brain and step away from limiting beliefs and mindsets. This will lead you to discovering your passion. (You don't need to search for it, it's already within you, you just need to discover it through self-love and self-awareness.)

All I am asking you to do is to make a commitment to yourself.

Take a piece of paper and re-write the following lines while saying them out loud. You can even manually create a few copies, and stick them in your wallet, in your office, in your fridge, on your wardrobe, etc.

I AM my biggest support.

I am committed to shining my truth.

I am committed to getting into alignment.

I am committed to making a difference in the world.

I choose to shift. I choose inner love.

I AM.

I CAN.

I am and I can love myself.

I love myself. I do.

I AM. I AM. I AM.

INTRODUCTION - WHY SELF-LOVE IS THE ONLY WAY

Through this book, we will follow a very specific process that consists of these steps:

Step #1 Emotional Peeling – We will dive deep to release self-guilt, low self-esteem and disempowering limiting beliefs. You will no longer feel like you have to constantly push because you're not feeling deserving and you need to constantly prove to yourself and others what you're capable of. Instead, we will get rid of negative emotions that are holding you back and that lead to habits that you know are not serving you on your journey. That step alone will help you feel so much lighter and you will never feel like a failure again.

Step#2 Why You Never Fail (removing fear) -This one is one of my favorites, especially when I get someone to do it via a 1:1 interaction. I can just feel that person's energy shift. However, I have the same intention for you, my reader. Wherever you're coming from and whatever obstacles you've had to overcome, I believe in you. And I know you deserve to love yourself more and give yourself more credit.

That step will help you look at your achievements in a totally new way. You will be able to make friends with your emotions and celebrate those little wins. You will also learn how to re-wire your brain in such a way that the word "failure" will be totally erased from your vocabulary.

Step #3 Control Your Precious Mind- This will help you to get rid of influences, people and marketing messages that don't serve you while attracting the exact guidance you need for your unique journey.

You will learn how to decide for yourself and that alone will help you make powerful shifts that are totally in alignment with who you are and what makes you happy. That step will help you get rid of ego that is designed to follow the masses.

You will ask yourself, *Do I need it in my life? Is it good for me?*

INTRODUCTION - WHY SELF-LOVE IS THE ONLY WAY

Many people who go through this step feel inspired to step into their unlimited courage, move to another city, or even abroad, or change their career or take on a new passion project.

You will no longer feel held back by, "Oh, but someone told me I would never be able to do it" or by someone who says it's not possible, or by what will others think.

Super powerful.

Step #4 Hidden Tricks to Identify and Get Rid of Limiting Beliefs That Are Holding You Back from Loving Yourself- Live your life the way it was meant to be lived- full of joy. You will learn how to re-wire your brain, level up your self-talk and that simple trick to transform the *"I can't's", and "I don't know how's"* into meaningful action that creates the reality you want.

Step 4 and chapter 4 will finish off with a motivational technique that will help you think beyond yourself, your mission, your purpose. The work you are meant to be doing. The work that gives you the abundance, not only financial but also an abundance of health, vitality and fulfillment.

That will lead us to another powerful step that will help you re-balance your heart chakra, which is a very powerful chakra to help you feel loved, love yourself and love others.

Step #5 Expressing Kindness

Self-love and loving others are interconnected. By allowing yourself to be kind, in an authentic way, you also give yourself the permission to be kind and help other people.

This step will show you and inspire you. It's a very simple set of actions you can do daily to unleash the gate to love and self-love. It will instantly shift you to higher vibrations and you will be able to manifest truly amazing people, things and circumstances, totally out of the blue.

INTRODUCTION -WHY SELF-LOVE IS THE ONLY WAY

Step #6 Creative Self-Expression to Love Yourself

That step will help you awaken your throat chakra so that you can express love and self-love while continuing to attract more and more of it on a daily basis.

The flow of love and self-love will be abundant when you commit to sharing what you know with other people. It's a very powerful step that connects to the abundance mindset.

Most people overlook it and some fear that this information should not be shared. Some are worried it may reach people who have bad intentions. However, this information can only be used for the highest good. Love and self-love are the highest good and expressing them in your own unique way, exactly the way you desire will help you to keep magnifying the life changing benefits of self-love.

From there, your life will be transformed forever.

Oh, and don't worry. This step will offer many options, both for extroverts as well as introverts. Your personal preference will be taken into consideration.

This step may also connect you with a new career opportunity that is more aligned with your passion. Knowing how to step into your passion and turn it into something that helps other people while adding value to their lives is the best way to step into abundance.

Step #7 Creating Super Positive Reminders for Lasting Inspiration

This handbook is not meant to be read once and forgotten about.

That is why Chapter 7 will show you multiple ways to create beautiful self-love reminders you can use to keep vibrating higher and higher while loving yourself more and more.

Through this step we will be diving deeper into Magnetic Attraction.

After all, this book is called *Self-Love Handbook – Magnified with Law of Attraction*, right?

INTRODUCTION - WHY SELF-LOVE IS THE ONLY WAY

We have some work to do here, the most meaningful and fun work ever!

Step #8 Action and Attraction

After getting rid of negative patterns and destructive emotional layers and stepping into self-love and different ways of deepening and strengthening it, we will have a look at magnifying everything with LOA.

That is what makes this book different. It's a holistic combo of the Law of Attraction and self-love.

Each step amplifies and magnifies the previous one. And so, step 8 will take step 7 to a whole new level.

You will discover some missing pieces to manifesting and learn how to combine the Law of Attraction with the Law of Action in a meaningful and powerful way. You will intuitively know how to create balance between action and attraction. Thanks to that balance you will never burn out. For example, too much action and pushing never ends well, I can tell you that. I have already shared my story and how I ended up with a complete mental, emotional and physical burnout.

At the same time, focusing entirely on attraction without taking meaningful and inspired action can leave us powerless. The most effective way is to combine attraction with action in a holistic, balanced way. By the time you get to that step you will know how to create the balance and peace of mind you have been seeking.

Finally, readers' transformation, and inspirational results they can pass on to their loved ones and their communities are my biggest passion, mission and drive.

After writing my last book, *Law of Attraction to Make More Money*, success stories came quickly to my email box. It helped many people. I also received valuable feedback where a reader mentioned: "In your next book, can we get something simple to follow? Something we can do in our free time and something that becomes a

INTRODUCTION - WHY SELF-LOVE IS THE ONLY WAY

process?" That really got me thinking. Eventually, I got connected to an idea that really excited me. What if I could add some healing recipes? And rituals and self-healing formulas? The final pages of this book contain a bonus-my best recipes that I use to align and treat my body and mind with love. There is also a weekend plan you can do to fully recharge.

I even included my favorite plant-based recipes. I love plant-based food as it makes me feel good and more aligned. Whether you decide to eat that way all the time, or want to try it part time, I am sure you will find at least a few healthy, healing recipes to add to your wellness routine. When it comes to healthy eating, it's very important to listen to your body and treat it with respect. But you don't want to overthink and over-worry about food as that creates resistance.

Then, there is also a simple morning and evening ritual you can follow.

The most important thing is to listen to your body. Give it what it needs but don't try to be perfect. Feel free to pick and choose.

I am very excited for you. Aside from the reasons I have already mentioned in the intro, I know that the transformation and wisdom you will unleash with self-love will help you inspire those around you.

-Your children will be able to benefit from self-love and feel empowered at school. That power will protect them in such a way that they will not be affected by negative comments, unfair teachers or anyone who's trying to project their own self-hatred onto them. One of my personal goals is to help children and teenagers enjoy their school years free of judgment, bullying and negative patterns while unleashing self-love, creativity and motivation. That will allow them to step into amazing careers that they love and feel inspired about, careers that align with their unique talents, personality and vocation.

INTRODUCTION -WHY SELF-LOVE IS THE ONLY WAY

-If you are a manager or lead any group of people, your work environment will be radically transformed. Self-love connects to self-leadership. As a result, you will be able to become a truly inspiring and authentically charismatic leader that people will want to follow and who they will benefit from following.

-Your personal relationships will be improved. People will notice your inner peace and will feel inspired.

Thank you once again for taking an interest in this book.

Please prepare a journal, or a notebook that you can use as you go through this book. You can also use one of the Law of Attraction journals I have made for you that go along with this book.

You will find them at:

www.LOAforSuccess.com/journals

Now, let's dive into it. We have some awesome work to do.

Chapter 1 Step #1 Emotional Peeling

It's time to dive deep to release self-guilt, low self-esteem and disempowering limiting beliefs. Thanks to this chapter, you will no longer feel like you have to constantly push because you're not feeling deserving and you need to constantly prove to yourself and others "what you're capable of".

Instead, we will get rid of negative emotions that are holding you back and that lead to habits that you know are not serving you on your journey. That step alone will help you feel so much lighter and you will never feel worthless again.

You will also come to a conclusion about what people, events and circumstances could have made you feel like you were not worthy. You will be able to let go of them all while protecting yourself from similar circumstances happening again.

Just like with healthy diets...they usually start with some kind of a detox, right? Imagine a person who's constantly eating processed food and fast food and then once a week, tries to eat a salad and drink a vegetable juice. It wouldn't work. It's important to dive deep and follow a smart plan, like we are doing here.

At the same time, perfection does not exist. Just like with healthy diets and eating, you don't need to constantly torture yourself and deprive yourself. Because that is not healthy either. It all comes down to focusing mostly on clean food and having little "cheats" every now and then. They will not make a big difference as long as they do not form a part of a negative pattern that gets triggered by a lack of self-love or some emotional trauma that needs healing.

Your emotional and spiritual wellness is the same. It's not about thinking 100% positively or trying to be a perfect, enlightened and highly self-developed (through self-improvement, that by the way later in this book, we will be looking at closely and debunking some myths of this industry too).

CHAPTER 1 EMOTIONAL PEELING

First, you need to "detox" that's for sure. Get rid of layers that no longer serve you. It's like emotional and spiritual "juicing". Then, we get on a healthy and balanced emotional "clean food diet". We are not perfect, but we are super happy with any progress. And, if every now and then we have that piece of pizza as a treat, everything is fine. We do not feel guilty. We feel like we chose that pizza, the pizza did not choose us.

Same with our emotional journey. There will be some emotions that are considered negative or not healthy, and some days will be like that, but they will no longer lead to a downward spiral or destructive habits.

You will be reacting in a different way because you will be empowered by a healthy dose of self-love, feel balanced and totally in alignment with how you feel.

Negative emotions are just feedback. Through the chapters of this book, you will get so high on the vibration of self-love, that your perception will change. And that is a balance that we want to create.

So that was step one- a little detox and emotional peeling before embarking on healthy, balanced, emotionally clean food diet.

The biggest layer to get rid of is the one of self-guilt.

The question is, has your mind ever been exposed to any of the following lines or concepts?

- Suck it up, it's all your fault.

- You are responsible for that.

- You are negative and because of that you always manifest negative things!

- Don't complain, just admit it's your fault.

My reply is: Really?

CHAPTER 1 EMOTIONAL PEELING

How can people who say those lines damage someone's self-worth with those disempowering words? How can someone lead someone into a downward spiral of self-hate or self-guilt by making them feel worse and worse? Unfortunately, these lines are very often quoted in the self-help, spiritual and entrepreneurial communities. But...they are not helping anyone...they can only make things worse. While most people will blindly nod at their leader and say, "Yes, you are right, it's all my fault", and they will pretend it's now all okay, deep inside they will feel a huge pain and discomfort. They will feel judged and misguided. That hidden self-guilt will remain buried in the subconscious mind until one day it will come back to surface, typically triggered by something little and innocent.

Like you burn your dinner, and your kid, spouse or roommate says, "It's your fault, you didn't pay attention", or you get a fine because you parked your car wrong and a friend says, "You should have checked". Boom....and suddenly you start feeling guilty about everything just because five years ago some leader suggested you need to hide your emotions and pretend like it's all fine.

Some people may even feel misled and then, again, they will feel guilty for following a given leader who got them on such a destructive path.

Why is the "it's all your fault, suck it up" approach wrong? And what approach can we follow instead?

Here's a simple example. It's just like a rebellious teenager. Yea, you can keep nagging them:

- Why you cut your hair like that?

- Why do you smoke?

- Why this and that? Why can't you just be like other kids?

Ask any therapist, or even someone with a minimal knowledge of psychology or compassion. They will all tell you that it's all about understanding how things work on a deeper level.

CHAPTER 1 EMOTIONAL PEELING

Unfortunately, we have all been conditioned to think the following:

- *I am always wrong.*
- *I am not good enough.*
- *It's my fault.*
- *Yea, I was there, I need to suck it up.*

We were mistakenly told that not admitting that it's all our fault means that we are in a victim mentality and because of that we will be pushed away. Whereas the opposite is actually true.

We step into the victim mentality by refusing to dive deep and having the courage to question certain mainstream beliefs, opinions of certain communities and the brainwashing of certain leaders and authorities.

At the same time, some people confuse empowerment with entitlement. These are two different things. A person with an entitlement mindset refuses to learn or to step into any kind of spiritual growth or self- awareness. They don't want to do any work and they believe that everything should be given to them. Now, I don't mean to be judgmental, I used to have that mindset too. Especially when I faced extreme poverty and had to live on the government's money. So, this mindset is something I can relate to.

Luckily, self-entitlement is a state of mind that can be healed through self-love and self-empowerment.

What makes self-empowerment different to self-entitlement is that a self-empowered person has the courage to seek guidance. The feeling of self-guilt is transformed into self-awareness and self-discovery. The necessity to feel responsible is outshone by the feeling of gratitude and transforms "It happened to me" to "It happened for me."

(The concept of "It didn't happen to you, it happened for you", is something I learned from Tony Robbins. His teachings really helped me when I was struggling with depression and difficult moments).

CHAPTER 1 EMOTIONAL PEELING

In order to illustrate my point, and show you how you can easily shift to self-love while still maintaining a healthy touch with reality I want to share some real-life examples, from different friends and mentees of mine.

For example, Jerry spent many years feeling depressed which led him to drugs and alcohol. Jerry used to run a marketing company with two other business partners. The business venture sounded very lucrative and was aimed at helping small businesses with online marketing using Facebook ads and SEO (Search Engine Optimization). It was when online marketing was still new, and Jerry was very excited to be starting a company in that field.

Jerry partnered with two business associates and invested lots of his personal money into the business. He had a lot of faith in that business and felt very positive about it, even though his wife felt skeptical and didn't like his business associates. However, Jerry had a vision of making lots of money, building a house and starting a family. For these reasons he decided to make a few "little sacrifices". He thought it would only be temporary and once the business was well set up, he would be able to create an abundant lifestyle for his family.

Jerry was mostly doing sales calls and customer service, while his business associates were supposed to deliver the marketing services for his clients. Every day Jerry drove 2 hours to their office and worked there for between ten and twelve hours.

Long story short- even though the business started off very well, the business associates took advantage of Jerry's trust as soon as they could. They got involved in some illegal activities, manipulated him into signing a few documents and disappeared, leaving him with a 100k debt.

That left Jerry feeling devasted. Not only was he in debt, but he also felt deeply frustrated about the money and time he had invested into the business. He felt powerless and taken advantage of. That led him to drugs and alcohol. His wife left him.

CHAPTER 1 EMOTIONAL PEELING

Even though Jerry quickly managed to find himself a well-paid job, moved back with his parents and started paying off the debt, he still felt haunted by the failure of his business.

He attended a few seminars, seeking answers. And BOOM, that only made it worse. One seminar was related to a wealthy mindset and the guru told him, "Hey, you were there, you signed the documents, you invested that money, suck it up and move on! It's all your fault!"

Then, Jerry attended a spiritual LOA seminar where the guru told him, "You attract what you are, change yourself and you will change your life, don't be so negative, you are in a very negative, victim mentality place!"

And then Jerry went to a happy motivational seminar where he was told, "Hey, just be happy, life is so amazing, just be grateful!"

All of this left him confused and he decided not to seek help from the gurus. Instead he decided to do some research and turned to books and videos to see what other people, who have been through hard and destructive times, had done to heal themselves.

He turned to meditation, quantum physics and many other self-help fields. He kept going through all those materials, rejecting most of it, feeling very disappointed and let down.

One video he watched introduced him to the concept of self-love and the subconscious mind. That really helped him and got him onto the path of self-love. The path of self-love helped him change his self-talk and that led him to what I like to call "self-engineered thinking" (more on that and how you can use it too, in a second).

Today Jerry has a prosperous career as a life coach. He can now market his new business very well. In fact, he's also an expert in helping other people get more business. He has four beautiful children and a wife who supports him through the good and the bad. He also has a trustworthy team for his business. How did it happen?

It all started with a simple mindset shift that Jerry made. He kept asking himself, "What am I supposed to learn from all this? What is the path I am supposed to discover? What is my purpose? How can I transform my suffering into something meaningful?"

Instead of saying, "Why am I such a loser? Why am I such a moron? Why didn't I check those documents?" he switched to, "What is this situation telling me? Where am I supposed to go? Where does my new, bright future start? What do I need to do to transform?"

Every day he kept asking his subconscious mind:

-How can I love myself more? How can I forgive myself? How can I be at peace?

-How can I feel better and more empowered?

-What is the number one thing I need to change?

These are all empowering questions and our subconscious mind is a truly amazing tool. Please note that there aren't any specific questions you need to ask, it's all up to you. What's important here is to ask questions that are positive.

Instead of asking, "Why do bad things always happen to me?" or "Why do I always attract bad people?" better questions are: "How can I attract positive people?" and "How can I learn empowering lessons from the past?"

Instead of saying, "Why are all the gurus the same and just want to get my money?" you ask, "How can I manifest a person, a mentor, who can really help me?"

"Where can I find a mentor who will understand me and guide me on my journey?"

"How can I attract a woman/man who loves me for who I am and not for the money I make?"

"How can I meet that person?"

CHAPTER 1 EMOTIONAL PEELING

So, Jerry started playing around with that. He would write his questions down or say them out loud, very often while driving, or at home while looking at the mirror. As I have already explained, these are not entitlement mindsets, these are empowering self-love mindsets.

People with self-love and self-empowering mindsets step into Courage and Patience. Those people understand that deep manifestations take time and they are okay with that. They enjoy the process and they feel that something unexpected is bound to happen. That deep faith and belief keeps them going.

A person with a self-entitlement mindset is deep into resistance. By constantly claiming that it's all about them, that everyone is wrong and that they need everything as soon as possible, they put extra stress on resistance. Again, I have been there too, I was looking for quick fixes. I am not judging, so please interpret this paragraph as me talking to my younger self.

Your subconscious mind is like a search engine. Some research may take time. Not all the topics you search for on Google or YouTube immediately give you the answers. Sometimes you may find the piece of content or a product you were looking for on page five, while what popped up first in your research wasn't really serving you. Still, it may have given you an idea and an introduction to the topic.

So, in the case of Jerry, he started off with empowering questions and stimulated his "positive search engine". He did that while getting rid of self-guilt and "Yo, bro, just suck it up, you were there, you wired the money, you hired those scammers, you partnered up with them, it's your fault!" Jerry was able to step into self-love.

And yes, men deserve self-love too and that is why I am writing about this case. While it's mostly women who read and research the topic of self-love, men are also invited to explore this field.

Self-love is empowering and can be used to enrich both feminine and masculine traits. I am getting off the topic a bit here, I know!

CHAPTER 1 EMOTIONAL PEELING

Everyone deserves self-love and it can only help us unleash the best. It works both for women and men so if you are a man reading this, you should not feel ashamed nor you should feel like hiding this book. You should feel proud.

Like Jerry...

So, here's how his story ended.

As Jerry kept asking himself those empowering questions, one day, on a pretty random drive where he was exploring a new job opportunity, one simple idea struck him. He decided he wanted to quit drinking and drugs. Most people didn't know he had an addiction problem. After all, he had a full-time job in sales. He looked all right, like a normal working human being, not some homeless drunk in the park. But every night he would drink at the bar and on weekends he would resort to cocaine and marijuana. That was his way to ease the pain. To release the self-guilt. To stop thinking about the past.

So, after positively brainwashing himself with positive questions, he asked himself, "What if I could stop drinking? What if I could stop doing drugs?" His ego went like, "But come on. As the loser that you are, you deserve your treats. It's fun, you meet girls, you meet people. You have a good job. Soon you will be able to pay off your debt, move out of your parents' home and get your own apartment, you're good. Why not enjoy evenings and weekends?"

But that enlightened self-love voice went like, "But what if I could stop drinking? Would I save more money? Would I be able to take another job, pay off my debt faster and help my parents?"

There was a bit of an internal struggle going on. One day as he was having a coffee, he saw an AA (Alcoholics Anonymous) ad which inspired him to join the local AA meeting. Long story short, that was where he met his new wife. It was where he quit drinking and drugs. It was where he decided to take another job. It was where he got inspired to help other people and learned many valuable mindset lessons.

Today, if you ask Jerry how he got where he's at- a successful life coach with his own passion-based business- he will tell you, "I decided to become a life coach because of the inspiration I got from AA.

AA taught me a lot about mindset and self-reflection. I was able to set up a business successfully because of the extra skill I got from the second job I used to do to pay off my debt. That taught me a lot about work ethic and discipline and improved my sales skills. I was able to market my business because of the SEO and Facebook ads skills I acquired from my failed business. Even though it was mostly my ex-business associates' job, very often I would stay in the office late to follow up with clients, checking the quality and that led me to research. I didn't even know I had skills that were transferable until I started my new, passion-driven business. It turns out that my "failed" business, hadn't really failed.

I wasn't failing, I was practicing.

"Oh Jerry, and how did you learn to hire people and teach other people how to be successful?"

Jerry said, "Well, because of the shady business associates who taught me a very valuable life lesson a few years ago."

"Oh, and what about your new wife, Jerry?

Jerry replied, "We met via AA, and we shared the same path, goal and journey to self-healing. We built our new selves through the power of self-love."

Wow, self-love, what a life-changing concept!

Now, here's a very powerful exercise for you.

Think of one thing you are very grateful for. It can also be an event or a person. Now, go back. What happened before that? And before that? And even before that? Go back to a certain painful moment from a few years ago. The moment that is no longer painful to you. Had you known what you know now, would you have felt pain?

Allow yourself to release the feeling of self-guilt. You were not failing, you were practicing!

Stop saying, "It's my fault, I need to suck it up."

Keep saying, "What can I learn?"

"What can I do to grow stronger?"

"How can I use my pain to help other people?"

These are all very empowering questions. Remember that your brain is a search engine, so be careful what you're typing in.

Fair enough, sometimes life gets hard and we don't achieve all our goals. Nobody has a perfect formula; some goals take longer. But there is always a meaning to that.

For years, I was told that the only way for me to share my message was by offering courses so I embarked on that path. I invested lots of money in coaching. One coach even told me I should never try to write, because nobody would read my books anyway. How disempowering is that?

Still, I learned how to communicate and how to organize my thoughts. When I decided to stick to my passion and go full time with my writing, it felt so light and so freaking right.

Firstly, because I finally felt like I was on my path. Secondly, because I realized how bad it feels when other people, aka leaders and authorities, talk down to you instead of understanding you, your unique gifts and talents and motivating you to follow your path.

I made a promise to myself to be a writer who shares empowering and uplifting messages and who focuses on unleashing the best in my readers without ever telling them what they should do. That is why I feel grateful for that ex-coach who wanted to get me on a different path.

I assume he's also under someone's negative influence and still hasn't broken free of them, hence his career and teachings are not authentic. Not judging, I have been there too. I know the pain. And I tell you what, self-love always leads to passion.

Talking of which, I have another inspiring, self-made, self-love success story to share!

Another friend of mine, Monica, is a passionate health coach who is helping people in her local community to shop, cook and eat organic, nourishing foods. She looks vibrant, fit and inspired.

But it wasn't always like that.

Monica grew up in a foster home and never met her parents. As a teen she quickly got onto the path to self-destruction. It was when she was at her lowest that she started seeking information on meditation. She had a friend who had quit drugs thanks to meditation. As she was watching videos about meditation, she stumbled upon a video about self-love. That sparked her interest and she started asking herself empowering questions. For example, for years, she had been led to believe:

- "You are nobody, nobody wants you nobody loves you, your parents never wanted you."

- "It's because something is wrong with you, suck it up, own it, be responsible for it, right?"

But thanks to self-love, she decided to step into her light and look for her purpose. For years she thought that the only way that could take her out of poverty was winning the lottery, inheriting some unexpected money, or possibly marrying someone rich.

She discouraged herself with disempowering lines like:

-I never went to college, what can I offer?

-I am not educated enough.

-All the jobs I can get are low paid jobs.

CHAPTER 1 EMOTIONAL PEELING

-I can't save lots of money anyway, so what I have left, I am better off spending it on drugs. At least then I can hang out with some cool people and feel like I have something to look forward to.

Remember though, your brain is a search engine. Start typing in questions that will lead you to answers you are searching for. Don't close yourself off with negative patterns and questions.

So, Monica started asking empowering, self-love questions:

- How can I love myself more?

- How can I meet people who really love me?

- What do I need to change in my life in order to be happy?

- Who can I ask for guidance?

So, here's what happened. As Monica was asking herself those healthy, empowering questions, she started coming up with positive ideas. She decided that the number one thing she needed to sort out was her health. She decided to quit drinking and drugs. She figured out that her party friends were not the best influence for her. So, instead, she decided to find another part time job at the weekends, because that way, she would keep herself busy, save up more money, and stop hanging out with people who didn't really care about her.

And this is what she did. During the week, she worked 9-5 in a simple admin job, then spend her free time learning about self-love, reading positive books and listening to podcasts. She started exercising and eating healthily which led her to transforming her body. She started making new friends at a local gym.

Eventually she realized that she was passionate about health and wanted to help other people embrace self-love by helping them transition to a healthy lifestyle. She really wanted to become a certified nutritionist but the courses she was looking at were very expensive.

But she kept asking those questions. One night she could not sleep. She was filled with a weird excitement and a feeling of, "Change is near" mixed with a bit of fear, "What if I never make it?"

That led her to watch some uplifting videos, and as she went into the internet rabbit hole, she came across a blog by someone who really inspired her. She stumbled upon an article that a blogger had finished off with a question: "What is your goal, and what is holding you back? Leave me a comment and I will help you."

She left a comment saying, "I want to be a health coach and nutritionist. I am already working two jobs to save up. My fear is that I will never be able to pay for my certification, and even if I do, it will be scary for me to leave my job."

Leaving that comment somehow made her feel better and she went to sleep. She woke up an hour earlier than her normal wake up time felling a bit anxious. She thought, *Oh no, I will go ahead and remove that comment, I probably come across as a complainer anyway*. She got up, started making her coffee and had a look at her phone only to see a notification that a blogger had replied to her saying, "What if you could start living your passion, in some way, shape or form, and feel that vibration even before you get your official certification? You seem to be working hard and on a good track. Some things do take time. Like, it takes nine months to have a baby. Even if you tried to get nine women and gave them one month each, it would still take nine months."

That gave Monica a lot to think about. So, she started asking herself, "How can I help someone and live my passion now?"

A few days after, as she was driving back from work, she noticed there was a new smoothie place opening in her town, and they were looking for staff. Passion for health was definitely an advantage.

Monica applied and got a part time job there at the weekends. She let go of her other part time job at the gas station as she was more excited about that smoothie place.

CHAPTER 1 EMOTIONAL PEELING

That job paid a bit better and was more fun to do. Monica got to learn a lot about healthy smoothies and herbs. People who visited that place were all health-oriented.

A few weeks afterwards, Monica met an elderly lady who was looking for someone who could keep her company, clean her house and cook her healthy meals. She really liked Monica's story, her drive, passion and perseverance. Eventually, she hired Monica and offered her a really good salary. That led Monica to quit her day admin job. By taking care of that old lady, she could make almost the same money and free up lots of her time so that she could follow her passion and become a health coach.

I believe that old lady was Monica's manifestation messenger, her angel in a way. These always come to help us, eventually. Be patient and start asking yourself empowering questions. One day, all that pain and suffering will make sense. Stop beating yourself up.

Now, it's your turn. Give yourself some self-love. Think of a problem or an issue you would like to solve. Maybe it's a past trauma, or some feeling of self-guilt. It's time to let go of that now.

Think of your self-talk. What are the negative questions, negative affirmations and patterns you keep telling yourself? How can you transform them into positive questions instead?

Even if the questions seem out of the gate, and very high level, you deserve to love yourself enough to ask those questions. So, go ahead and do it now. Whenever your mind starts to wander, or you feel down, ask yourself:

What can I do to feel better now?

How can I raise my vibration?

What can I do to eat healthy food and enjoy it?

What can I do to let go of...?

What did I learn from...?

CHAPTER 1 EMOTIONAL PEELING

How can I attract someone who can help me...?

Chapter 2 Step #2 Making Friends with Your Emotions on a Deeper Level

I'll be really blunt here. You need to give yourself more credit.

Whatever it is that you're doing, you are not giving yourself enough credit. How do I know? Because I am "guilty" of the same thing. And it's something I am still learning how to get rid of, every day.

Why do we think it's bad to give ourselves credit? And why does it bother me to see people (myself included) who don't give themselves enough credit?

First of all, the real culprit here is mainstream society's brainwashing. You know, it goes like this: "Don't stand out, be like everyone else. If you excel at something, other people may feel bad about themselves."

The problem with that? People lose motivation to do anything or really enjoy what they do.

Yes, I think it's very important to stay humble. And do the work you were meant to be doing while really taking your time to do it well, and with passion. Also, when you do the work that is really authentic and aligned with your highest calling and you take inspired action from the place of self-love (not self-interest), then what you do is also meant to inspire other people.

And that deserves credit.

However, before we start looking at the bigger picture and focusing on your work, whether it's pure passion, hobby or something you are doing professionally, it's good to start small. Why not have a look at all those little events and mini achievements when you achieved your goal?

CHAPTER 2 MAKING FRIENDS WITH YOUR EMOTIONS

Go back to your childhood. Maybe it was your first swim (sorry, mine was traumatic I don't have any achievements there, but I am still happy I jumped into that pool).

Or that feeling when you rode your bike for the first time.

Or when you went on your first date. What about getting your driving license? What about your first vacation or a trip you enjoyed?

Finally have a look at all those little wins and moments of joy and happiness. How did they feel? Take a piece of paper and write them all down. Love yourself, and every cell of your body for those achievements.

Love yourself for even attempting to do something and taking action. Even if you didn't finish the project, please be good on yourself. At least you started.

Believe it or not, two years ago I began writing a book on confidence. The writing process was on and off because I was going through many emotional and spiritual shifts and when they happened, I always felt compelled to go back to the manuscript and make changes. Eventually, I started beating myself up that one book project was taking so long. On one hand, I was beating myself up that I was so slow and lacked confidence in myself. Then I was beating myself up thinking:

If I can't even finish that book project about confidence, what kind of a person I am? Even when I put it out, I will feel fake.

And so, the book got forgotten somewhere on my computer.

Finally, I joined a group of other writers who also happened to have the same problem. One writer admitted he had dozens of book projects like this, half-finished and abandoned. Another one said, "Yea, that always happens if you are a self-help writer and you want to be putting out books that are authentic. So, get used to it. Most of your manuscripts will never be ready to publish, I hear ya Elena!"

CHAPTER 2 MAKING FRIENDS WITH YOUR EMOTIONS

It would go on and on. Now, while I do believe that most of my writer friends had very good intentions, and wanted me to feel understood, eventually I got very stuck in my own mindset.

I was beating myself up for spending two years on writing on and off something I could not even publish or show to anyone. I started seeing that confidence book as a failed project and started feeling fake as well. In the meantime, I also began working with a mentor, who basically told me I should abandon that project and maybe focus on something else or simply focus on some main stream hot topics and put my writing in there.

That was even worse, because for me, if I lack passion for something, I am not productive.

Where am I going with my story?

Well, it all changed when I began applying what I am teaching you in this chapter. Giving myself credit for every little micro step and action I had taken throughout my entire life.

I remember getting started on this exercise. I got myself a fresh journal (I am extremely hooked on journaling) and sat down in a coffee shop drinking a delicious matcha latte. And I began writing in that journal like a mad woman. Giving myself more credit, loving myself more.

Believe me or not, I was there writing my thoughts down for at least a few hours. Focusing on having gratitude for every little achievement in my life, even things I no longer value, because I had taken for granted, for example, learning how to drive.

My nephew is just getting started on his learning how to drive journey. For him it's a big thing. Most of his friends are already driving around. That's all they talk about. Will he be next? Most of his actions, thoughts and what he talks about focus on driving. I was able to give him courage and help him, because I have been there as well.

CHAPTER 2 MAKING FRIENDS WITH YOUR EMOTIONS

That again amplified my gratitude for my achievements, and for every little step on my journey.

Now please note, I don't want to come across as one of those authors who only write about themselves. Not my intention. I really want to illustrate my point and show you how one simple decision can totally transform your life.

As I began writing things down in my journal and giving myself more credit, my forgotten confidence book cropped up. And I got one more thought- *it was meant to happen.* I wasn't going to be a confidence author. That was not how I want to brand myself. I want to be known as a self-love and Law of Attraction author.

However, and this is a very big "however", when I got back home and began reading my old confidence manuscript, I realized that many of the concepts and thoughts I had written were something I could include in my other books. So I did.

That is why I managed to write my book *Law of Attraction to Make More Money* very quickly. The confidence book was like a gym that had helped me grow my muscle and many of the mindset shifts I had originally written in my never published book on confidence, helped me tremendously as I was writing my last book.

Conclusion:

You don't fail. You succeed or you learn.

Learning may take much longer than you originally envisioned, and this is totally fine. But, by going back to all your achievements, and really feeling them again and again, you enter a totally new vibration of freedom and creativity. You feel empowered again and everything makes sense. Not only that, but you also enter the vibration of being resourceful.

So, even though I never published that book on confidence, many parts from the original manuscript formed the skeleton for my book *Law of Attraction to Make More Money.*

CHAPTER 2 MAKING FRIENDS WITH YOUR EMOTIONS

What really made me excited were emails from the happy readers who read that book. The feedback like, "Thanks to your book I am learning to be resourceful", or "Thanks Elena, now I feel much more confident when it comes to manifesting money and abundance", or "The exercises helped me see things in a new light. I applied for a new job and I got it, I never thought that woo woo LOA book would help me feel more confident and motivated, but it did."

Exactly like I said in the intro. These are some of the positive effects of self-love (not self-interest). With self-love, there is no "pushing".

Also, whatever your occupation is, whether you are a business owner, work for the government, or are a student- when you give yourself more self-love and more credit, all from the place of the highest good for all, people will feel your transformed energy and they will be inspired.

That is why giving yourself credit, going way back to the past, and focusing on those little achievements will open another powerful gate to the best self-help tool ever- the tool of self-love.

Don't hide your gist, don't hide your achievements. Don't be afraid of anything that you do.

I used to be guilty of that too, don't worry. For example, I can write pretty fast. One of the reasons is that I only write about topics I am passionate about and know can help other people. Very often while talking to other authors or writers I felt a bit judged. "Really? You can write that many words a day? How is that possible?"

For a really long time, I didn't feel good about it. I even felt like hiding my gift. I felt like I would be rejected and ridiculed. Or that people would think I am crazy. However, going through this step of the self-love process made me realize that everything that we do must be celebrated. Using what we do to inspire other people in a positive way, always from the place of abundance and confidence, has a very transformative effect.

CHAPTER 2 MAKING FRIENDS WITH YOUR EMOTIONS

One of my mentors once told me, "People love motivation, but not from another motivational speech. What people really like and need is to see someone else do something they love and feel that energy. Because that energy helps them unleash their full potential and step into all their gifts that they can share with the world."

Everyone is different and everyone has different gifts. I stayed silent for a long time and I would allow myself to be a victim. A disempowered victim. I would allow everyone step on me and laugh at what I consider valuable assets I can share with the world through my writing.

For you, it may be something else. Please, don't hide it. Let it shine. There is someone out there who needs your gifts and your work. You are divine and what you bring to this world matters.

My motivation is

to empower you to the best of my ability. I don't want anyone to feel the way I used to feel- forgotten, unappreciated, laughed at. Nobody deserves to be treated this way. I made it my mission and my purpose to help you step into your highest light for the highest good, for you and those around you.

Allow yourself to be you and only you. Because only you can be you.

Now, I warmly invite you to take a powerful decision- take a few hours off. It could even be the whole day, if you have the time and opportunity to do it. It's time for you to go on a date. With you! Yes, only you and your self-love journal.

Schedule your self-love date in. Allow yourself to enjoy coffee, tea or a smoothie in your favorite place. Or go to the beach, or a park. Or even book a massage. Whatever it is that you enjoy doing. Perhaps, you feel like staying in and listening to your favorite music, while having a bath, and using aromatherapy candles or essential oils and sipping on your favorite tea.

CHAPTER 2 MAKING FRIENDS WITH YOUR EMOTIONS

If you're a woman (I know most of my audience is women), you can even get a nice make up and do your hair differently. Enjoy and when you do that, keep saying to yourself, "I love you!"

(But I will stress it again, I never intend my writing to be only for women, I believe many men can also benefit from some of my ideas).

Whatever your sex, origin, age or ethnicity is- Elena loves you!

Finally, whatever scenario you choose to do this step, be prepared for lots of writing in your journal.

Alternatively, if you don't like it, you can also record yourself on your phone and just share with yourself, what you are grateful for and all your achievements, both small, big and even the unfinished projects and attempts.

You will soon see they are not failed projects. They were valuable lessons that made you grow.

Personally, I prefer to write it all down in my journal, and then read through it several times. Reading through my own achievements makes me feel very, very good.

Sometimes, I even go as far as recording what I wrote. You can easily do it using your phone, or by downloading a program called Audacity (it's free as of now). You can record all your achievements and even play your favorite music in the background. Call me a crazy woman, but I do it all the time. Then, I re-listen to myself while on a walk, or in a gym, before I go to sleep, or even when I have a bad day. It's really an amazing self-healing therapy you can do whenever you want.

So please, go ahead and do it now. Stop reading this book and take a few hours off to celebrate this step.

If you're ready with this "assignment" (that word makes it sound a bit stiff, while it's supposed to be fun), and would like to share your experience with other readers, be sure to post a review. Your review may motivate other people in our community to take inspired action and experience the healing benefits of self-love by giving yourself the credit you deserve.

Trust me, something will change for sure! Come back to this step whenever you have a bad day. Heck, a friend of mine even writes things like, "I know how to say a few words in French", or "I know one yoga pose and what it's good for", or "I know how to make a nice green smoothie".

Everything counts. Everything matters. Whatever you have done is important and forms part of who you are and who you are becoming.

Chapter 3 Step #3 Control Your Precious Mind As If Your Life Depends on It Because It Does

There is a reason why this step is step#3 and not step #2 in this process. You see, it's easier to own your mind and eliminate other people's negative influences and opinions when you already know how to respect yourself, give yourself credit and celebrate your little wins.

Here's the sad truth: most marketing messaging you see out there is designed to make you feel bad and make you feel like you're not good enough. Because you are not making this amount of money, you haven't traveled to all those places, your kids are not perfect, your job is not perfect, and you haven't lost that final pound this week…we can go on and on and on.

If your mind is not 100% owned and controlled by you, it's very easy to get distracted.

On a positive note, there are also many good people who use social media to share positive and uplifting messages using light and good intentions.

I am not meaning to be negative. In this day and age, it's hard to be living like a hermit. There will always be an ad targeted at you. And again, some ads are meant to be shown to you as this is what you are meant to attract because what you discover will help and benefit you.

The question is- what will help you and what will not help you? How will you know?

The answer is self-love. When you own your precious mind, you focus on yourself and you fully believe on yourself, you will not be prone to attracting people and messages who want to benefit from you without providing you with the value that you might be seeking.

CHAPTER 3 CONTROL YOUR PRECIOUS MIND

By entering your sacred space of self-love, you enter a whole new vibrational state. The best way to go about it, is to keep asking yourself the following questions:

-Do those people (and messages) have good intentions?

-Where do I want to be in the next five years?

-What is my next exciting goal?

-Is that thing helping me get closer to that goal, or taking me further away from it?

Now, I am all for being positive. But you need to be positive in an authentic way and own your mind. You own your mind when you can think for yourself and make your own decisions.

When I was younger, I made lots of bad decisions because I didn't own my mind. I let my family and society tell me what to do. I allowed them to program my mind and then I was blindly making decisions that were not making me happy.

Then, I felt guilty. I wasn't happy, because I worked so hard for my "success", but it was only to realize that I worked hard to create a prison not freedom. In other words, I worked hard to create someone else's success, but not my own.

Things began to change a bit when I got on a path of self-help and began working with coaches and mentors. Unfortunately, I still wasn't in a self-love and *own your mind* mindset. As a result, I was easy prey for many of those people. I remember taking part in a small mentorship program related both to mindset and business. During one meeting, I felt compelled to express my intention about what I considered unethical and manipulative marketing methods that the course "mentor" we had was urging us to apply.

CHAPTER 3 CONTROL YOUR PRECIOUS MIND

You know what happened? I was called a hater, and someone who has "a poor person's mindset". The "mentor" added, "Elena, you have many limiting beliefs you need to work through."

I managed to get my power back, and replied, "A belief is limiting if it's limiting you and your personal growth. However, if that belief empowers you, it's not limiting. You cannot have a belief that both empowers you and limits you". And I left that "mastermind". Needless to say, the guy who was trying to teach me and mentor me is no longer in business. Because of his unethical practices, several individuals reported him to the authorities, and he lost everything.

I am very glad I followed my heart on that day, because only God knows what could have happened.

What I am trying to bring your attention to are patterns.

For example, personally, I felt disempowered. I lacked self-love and I would just move around across different communities and industries with no sense of belonging. No matter where I went, I felt extremely lost and attracted people who also felt lost, but their way of dealing with it was to make me feel worse about myself.

Eventually, though, I started attracting amazing books, videos and resources that helped me.

I am very grateful for a YouTuber Aaron Doughty. Not only because of his amazing videos but also because he recommended the book called *Reality Transurfing*, written by a Russian author, Vadim Zeland.

I am extremely grateful for this author and his teachings which are very relevant to this step. In his book *Reality Transurfing*, he talks about the concept of pendulums. A pendulum can be any collective energy or organization that gets into your mind to control it. That is the simplest way of explaining what a pendulum is. I would recommend the original book (you can also look it up on YouTube as the author generously posted the audio version for free, at least for the time being as I am writing this chapter, his book is up on his official YouTube channel in audio format).

As I was reading his book, which to be honest I have read several times and will read again, I found so many answers I had been searching for. His writing really brought tears of joy to my eyes. I finally realized how to let go of other people's negative influences that no longer served me.

On the other hand, there may also be positive pendulums, for example a community that brings joy into your life. Perhaps you go to a bookstore and you search for your favorite fiction author, because you know that thanks to his writing you will feel entertained and relaxed. Or maybe you listen to your favorite podcast or look for some specific and life changing information by following someone's blog, or a newsletter.

Whatever serves you, feels light and feels good helps you on your self-love journey. Self-love and self-awareness go hand in hand. By allowing yourself to make your own choices and walking away from things that no longer serve you, you stay connected to your inner wisdom and light.

Back to the concept of pendulums- a negative pendulum can be someone whom you perceive as an authority and who tells you to follow a certain path that is not good for you. It can be a mentor who's not offering the guidance that really helps you on a deeper level but is more driven by his or her own success and significance.

It can be doing something that everyone else is doing because you feel like it's expected of you.

In those moments, be strong. Give yourself the courage to be yourself. That doesn't mean you should start attacking those "pendulums." According to the author of the above-mentioned book *Reality Transurfing*, fighting pendulums is futile and only drains your energy.

CHAPTER 3 CONTROL YOUR PRECIOUS MIND

As I like to put it, the best way is to focus on yourself and your own path and shining your light with a strong intention of using that light to inspire those who need it.

The light can be any creative or passionate work you want to do, any professional work you would like to be doing to really feel fulfilled (this is like true ambition coming straight from your heart).

It could be volunteering for your local community or taking up a new hobby. It could even be something as simple as walking around with an apple or a smoothie, because you never know, someone might be passing by and they may get inspired. Maybe that person had a bad day and as a coping mechanism had the intention of getting some unhealthy food and alcohol on the way back home. But now they have seen you and have decided to drive by a healthy food store and pick a salad instead!

All your actions matter, as we discussed in the previous step (step #2 – where you were asked to give yourself more credit). Through this step it is time to get honest with yourself and identify people, events, even social media platforms, or very specific programs, social media channels and other media that you feel are no longer serving you.

We have already done the emotional peeling to release self-guilt in the very first step of this process. Now, what about maintaining that and taking care of what you put in your mind?

At the same time, please remember that everything is a learning experience. I could have felt guilty of allowing certain mentors into my life. I could have started calling them out on being manipulative and what not. But that would bring me back to the victim mentality. Instead, a wiser thing to do is to realize the following:

-There was a reason I allowed that person into my mind. It was supposed to be a learning experience to make me stronger.

-I forgive that person fully. They need to love themselves more and they also deserve self-connection.

CHAPTER 3 CONTROL YOUR PRECIOUS MIND

-I love myself and I forgive myself and others. I now send light and healing energy to that person and they can use it whenever they feel ready for their own self-love self-awakening. Until then, they can choose their own path and I no longer judge them.

-I allow myself to be me. I allow myself to choose wisely. I feed my mind with a healthy, natural clean food diet. This is for my highest good and for the good of my loved ones and my whole community.

Can you see and feel where it's going? It feels so much better to let go and feel empowered knowing that you can pick and choose what kind of messaging you decide to enter your mind.

Now, it's time to finish this chapter with an exercise. It will take less time than the exercise in the previous step. In fact, half an hour is totally fine.

On one piece of paper, or on a new page in your self-love journal, write down all the messages, people and negative influences that you are now ready to let go of.

Take a look at the page and start drawing little hearts around what you wrote.

Now, place both of your hands on your heart. Say, "I love myself and I love you. I love you and I love myself."

Repeat a few times. Then say, "I am now ready to release, I am now ready to let go. And I am forever grateful."

Now, on a second piece of paper write down what you are grateful for and what those negative messages and influences taught you.

It can be something simple like, "I learned who I don't want to be. I learned which path is not for me. I get closer to my divine wisdom and light, it made me who I am".

Again, draw little hearts around your gratitude statements, then again say, "I am ready to release, I am ready to let go and I am feeling light and grateful." If needed and if it feels good and therapeutic for you, repeat the process several times and keep writing.

To finish off, rip off the pages, or if you were writing on a piece of paper, start tearing it up. You can also burn it. Whatever feels right. You are now letting go of the past, while being fully in the present moment where all the possibilities exist. Now you can open your beautiful mind to new opportunities.

On another piece of paper, describe exactly what your life will look like in five years' time. Write it, as if you were seeing everything and feeling and experiencing everything.

Whatever comes to your mind, remember that you are here and now in the present moment where all the possibilities exist. You are now on the self-liberating journey of self-healing and self-love. You are now totally letting go of the past and past experiences. You are feeling lighter and more empowered. So, allow your mind to think big. Write down all the details about what your life will look like in the next five years.

Focus on where you want to live, what you want to do for a living and who you want to spend your time with.

Do you live in house or in an apartment? Which city? Do you travel a lot? Where do you work? Who do you work with? How much money do you earn per month? What do you eat? Where do you eat? What do you wear? Who do you surround yourself with? Do you have children?

Allow yourself to see and feel all the details. We are definitely working with the Law of Attraction here.

Finally, on a new piece of paper, write down the following questions:

-*Who can help me?*

-*Who do I allow to enter my mind?*

-*Who inspires me?*

CHAPTER 3 CONTROL YOUR PRECIOUS MIND

-Who motivates me?

-Who loves me? (You love yourself, and I love you too and many others love you too!)

-Who can teach me?

-Who can guide me?

-Who can mentor me?

If you already know your answers, start writing down the names of your potential guides, mentors and teachers.

Write down the books that you think can help you on your journey. Do you need to acquire new skills to help you tune into the new reality you are creating for yourself?

Whatever your vision is, self-love is an amazing amplifier, and without it, as you already know, it's very easy to get misled and start mistakenly manifesting other people's goals and desires. And you already know that the most important thing is to manifest your goals and your desires. That starts with self-love and authenticity.

Don't be afraid to let go of the influences that no longer serve you. They may have served you in the past, but if the next chapter in your life means you're ready for something new, it may also mean you are getting ready to let go.

Whenever in doubt ask yourself-how does it feel? Does it feel light or heavy?

Your gut knows the answer. Also, by installing your vision, the vision you now carry in your heart, the vision of you and your life in the next five years, you are connecting with your subconscious mind and your inner guidance.

You feel empowered to start asking yourself good questions, questions that heal your soul and guide all your actions.

CHAPTER 3 CONTROL YOUR PRECIOUS MIND

Remember Jerry, whom I mentioned in the first chapter of this book? He mastered the art of self-love by asking himself good questions. Those questions helped him leave the path of self-destruction and got him on the path of self-love, self-gratitude and self-discovery.

Now that you have your vision, your vision that you know is yours, you know where you're going. Whenever you're in doubt, as for who to listen to, or which influence aka "pendulum" is right for you, ask yourself this question: "Is it helping me get closer to or farther away from my vision?"

For example, if you set a vision for yourself that you want to be an actor or a writer, then mastering your craft is empowering and bringing you closer to your dream.

That means that in your free time, you naturally feel inspired to do what you love- acting or writing. It's who you are, and you love it. But, if a negative influence comes up, for example, your friends want to go out and get drunk, your inner mechanism might tell you this:

Is it really serving me? Tomorrow I will feel hangovered. Is it really worth it? What about signing up for those writing or acting classes?

That can allow you to connect with a new group of people who are exactly on the same journey as you are.

Likewise, if, on your vision, you prioritized your health and wellbeing and you said you eat healthy, nourishing foods and you love yourself, your weight and your energy, you will probably reject any kind of disruptive fast food marketing messages as negative influences or negative pendulums. Instead, you will naturally want to eat something healthy.

Finally, if your vision incudes a new profession, and deep inside you know it's a career that excites you, and a career that connects you with your passion, by asking yourself empowering questions you may get tempted to start saving up for college or any education or a diploma that may help you get closer to your desired career. Suddenly "sacrifices" will not feel like sacrifices because deep inside you will know you are making a good decision.

And even though everyone around you will be telling you, "It's not worth it, it's risky to change jobs, why not keep your old job?" or "It's hard to study and work full time," you will simply smile and reject those beliefs as negative pendulums that try to disconnect you from your truth and from who you really are.

I hope you're excited now. And it's time to dive into the next step.

I am also very curious to hear about your journey and experiences, so if you have a second, please share them by posting an honest review on Amazon. It will also help other people in our small community. Everyone loves to read about transformations. Other people's stories have much more value and motivation than just a pure *how-to* theory.

However, I will ask you to decide for yourself. If you're ready to share, please share, if not, wait for the right moment.

Chapter 4 Step #4 The Number One Self-Love Trick to Eliminate Limiting Beliefs and Self-Doubt

I am very excited for you, because in this chapter, we are going to re-wire your brain. We will cover that simple trick to transform "I can't do it" and "I don't know how" into meaningful action that creates the reality you want. You will feel positively surprised to see what you're capable of after going through this step.

Before we get into it, let's recall the process we have covered so far. I know for a fact that some of you have been doing the exercises diligently as you read each chapter.

But some of you just went ahead with reading, saying, "I will do the exercises later". How do I know? Because I am the second type of reader and I can totally relate! That is why it may be handy to go through a little recap.

If you did all the exercises after each chapter, you will be able to internalize the teachings on a deeper level. In case you skipped them-no worries. I don't want to interfere with your reading patterns. I know you will do the exercises whenever you feel ready and inspired to do them and you will know how to do them in your own, unique way. After all, everything happens for a reason.

In step #1 we learned how to get rid of self-guilt and how to move on and find the meaning of whatever negative happened to us. By erasing self-guilt, we release negative emotions and patterns and are ready for the new.

It's like the emotional detox. We also learned how to ask empowering questions and how to make friends with our internal search engine, that is- how to ask questions that connect us with our goals. That allowed us to shift away from being a victim to being a warrior.

CHAPTER 4 ELIMINATE SELF-DOUBT

In step #2 we learned how to value ourselves and give ourselves more credit. We dived very deep into all our accomplishments.

The transformative effect of chapter 2 is that we start to value any action we have taken, and we no longer see failure as failure. We succeed (on our terms) or we learn. That empowering mindset can instantly connect you with new habits and ideas to help you transform your spiritual life, your personal life and your career.

In step #3 we learned how to protect our minds from negative influences and why it's important to pluck up our courage and allow ourselves to let go of everything that no longer serves us. We even did a little ritual to release the last traces of self-guilt and through that ritual we felt lighter and lighter.

The ritual included listing all the negative influences and circumstances in our lives, finding something we learned from it, something we can be grateful for, sending them love and sending us love and letting them go.

Then, we created a vision for ourselves and where we want to be in the next five years. In alignment with that, we learned how to determine what actions, people and influences can help us get closer to that vision.

That helped us become more confident in taking meaningful and inspired action, totally in alignment with the Law of Attraction and fueled by self-love.

The best is yet to come. Because, in this chapter, we will learn how to erase self-doubt and limiting beliefs. A simple example: In the beginning, I struggled with writing this book. I kept saying that I didn't know how.

Even though I have written several books in the past, I felt stuck with this one. I felt so much resistance, and what you resist-persists.

CHAPTER 4 ELIMINATE SELF-DOUBT

If you keep telling yourself you *can't do* something, your subconscious mind will respond with just that and you will start receiving a "fake proof" of what you think is your reality.

You will start diving deeper and deeper into self-doubt and with that mindset, even if you see someone just like you doing what you would love to be doing, you might reject such an inspiration and say, "Oh but they had this and that, they had better connections, they had better education" and this and that.

How do I know? Because I was in that mindset for many years. Because of that I let many amazing opportunities slip by while witnessing other people's success stories.

I quickly realized they were doing something different and they were not really pushing that hard. They just knew what they wanted, really believed in it, and lived with the mindset, "I already got this, it's already mine". That mindset led them to taking small and inspired steps every day, and those actions didn't feel like work.

While it didn't take me lot of time to understand, it took me lots of time to be able to apply to my own life. One thing is to understand and tell yourself, yea, I know I need to do it, I really do. And another thing is to actually do it.

So, I went through a process of trial and error. One thing that helped me was my own self talk and internal dialogue. I was using the technique of empowering questions that I have already explained through sharing Jerry's story. Because of that I began eliminating resistance and I was able to start transforming all areas of my life.

For example, I had a limiting belief that having a healthy lifestyle is hard and complicated. That heathy food is very expensive, and that it takes hours to create healthy meals. I used to believe that working out and exercising are only for extremely motivated and fit people. I even thought that if I went to the gym I would be laughed at because as a kid, I had always been laughed at during the PE classes. Whether it was gymnastics, or a simple volleyball or basketball game, I had always been a victim there.

Knowing what I know now, I know why it was happening. Back then I was in self-hate and self-doubt and I would allow other people to create labels for me. I did not have the courage to obey, neither did I have the courage to transform on my own terms.

So, this is how it all started. My limiting beliefs about health and fitness originated from my childhood. In my family, nobody was healthy and many of my family members would laugh at people who jogged or got involved in any healthy activities. My grandpa would always say, "Oh those people have too much free time on their hands, maybe they are not working? When do they take care of their children?"

So, boom, my limiting belief got a strong consolidation.

If you work out, you don't take enough care of your family. If you work out too much you are not a good person. Working out is a waste of time. If you eat healthily it's too expensive and if you spend money on expensive stuff you are not a good person. Nobody will like you if they see how much money you spend. They will no longer connect with you. You will die anyway, you don't need to eat any healthy stuff.

That resulted in massive resistance. Several years ago, I still struggled with eating healthily and I could not lose weight. I tried different things but could never commit to a healthy lifestyle. My limiting beliefs and lack of self-love were a very harmful combination. I didn't know which direction to take, because wherever I went, I felt like a total failure.

It took me a while to understand where my limiting beliefs were coming from and why they were forming. It was because of the lack of self-love as well as allowing other people's opinions to enter my mind. And very often people with those opinions do not love themselves either or they just repeat what they have heard from others, acting like robots. If everyone is saying something it must be true, right?

CHAPTER 4 ELIMINATE SELF-DOUBT

Now, I don't mean to be judgmental, because I have been there as well. It was thanks to discovering the concept of self-love and going through all the steps I have already described, that I was able to identify the limiting beliefs that were holding me back.

The process I share in this book should be done in a certain way, exactly the way it is presented. Now, that you understand what self-love is and what is not, and how to use it for your and others' highest good, and how to protect your mind and ask empowering questions, this step will feel like a piece of cake.

However, had we entered this step at the beginning of the book, it may have felt a bit patronizing or even cookie cutter. Like a typical self-help book, yea, "Just get rid of those limiting mindsets that are holding you back and you will be fine."

But you and I know it's all a process. It's a deep work that we are doing here.

Back to my limiting beliefs. Once I had learned how to gradually get rid of them without feeling self-guilt and without feeling like a victim, I also understood that what very often holds people back is not the limiting beliefs themselves. Very often it's their feeling guilty about having them. Or creating another limiting belief: "I have a limiting belief, and this is who I am and I don't know how to get rid of it." The moment you start putting other "I can't" and "I don't know how's" on what is already stopping you from shining your light and reaching your full potential, you make it harder and harder.

However, once you understood the mechanism behind getting rid of limiting beliefs, you can easily apply it to all the areas of your life. This is exactly what I did. I started off with health and fitness. I realized that area needed most of my attention as I was transforming. I also knew that by creating a healthy lifestyle, I could resort to natural methods that would help me soothe the pain, feel less anxiety, sleep better and eat healthier.

Thanks to self-love, I quickly identified all those negative voices in my head as well as the limiting beliefs that were pretty much coming from other people and were installed on my hard drive.

But here's the caveat: you cannot just remove a limiting belief and hope for the best. You need to replace the limiting belief with an empowering belief.

For example, the beliefs I got from my family:

- "If you work out you don't have the time for your family."
- "Eating healthily is only for rich people."
- "Eating healthily doesn't taste good anyway, come on, you gotta have something good in your life. Life is already hard enough."

I began replacing these with self-love and empowerment, one by one. For example, instead of, "If you are always working out, you don't have the time for the family", I said, "You can both work out and hang out with the family and friends".

I began organizing hiking trips that were fun. I could get some of my friends and family members and we would just walk in nature, burn calories and have fun. We could still catch up, but instead of going to a bar, we would get some fresh air, admire nature or even join a yoga workshop. Then, eventually we felt inspired to combine our hikes with eating healthy food.

Aside from that, I realized that health is the most valuable asset we have. I can still remember what it felt like when I could not get up and felt absolutely powerless. The doctors would just prescribe antidepressants, but the truth is, my body lacked a healthy, clean diet and exercise.

Now, I have never been a gym person. So, I decided to focus on other activities, mostly in nature, like hiking, for example. Then I also joined yoga and Pilates classes. I added more positive changes gradually. I kept track of my progress. I still allowed myself to get off track every now and then. That is absolutely fine. You don't want to

CHAPTER 4 ELIMINATE SELF-DOUBT

be too strict on yourself. It's better to focus on your long-term vision.

Eventually, I started enjoying my hikes so much. Getting outdoors in the fresh air just felt amazing. I loved my hikes so much that I decided to take them to another level and I began jogging. Another change and shift added gradually. Had I vowed to jog every day at the beginning of my journey, I wouldn't have had any success with it. I would have worked on will power alone. And that can only last so long.

A friend of mine, who was going through the same process, decided to transform his health and fitness as well. Aside from that, he became very inspired by what I was doing with my writing. His challenge was time, because he had a full-time job and a family to support. But he managed to do it anyway. He started small. He started waking up ten to fifteen minutes earlier and doing some simple exercises that required no equipment. Just watching YouTube videos and following online fitness courses and DVDs.

He made a small commitment that only took fifteen minutes a day, every day, first thing in the morning, before things became too hectic.

His old limiting belief had been that if you had a full-time job and a family to support, and you wanted to be a good dad, you had to give up on your passions because continuing with them would be egoistical. He had heard it from his dad, his uncle, and his grandpa.

But the new, empowering belief, fueled by self-love was this:

"As a good dad, I need to take care of my health and fitness and set a good example to my family. This also allows me to be more productive at work and increase my chances of getting a promotion."

So, he kept going. Eventually, he started waking up even earlier and added more exercises to do in the morning because it felt so good. His wife also became inspired to do fitness training.

Then he decided to add another habit. While at work, he had a one-hour lunch break. He didn't need a full hour to eat anyway. He could enjoy his lunch within twenty minutes, and then instead of browsing through his phone, he decided to focus and write. He soon realized that half an hour a day can be easily turned into a thousand words. That's thirty thousand words a month which can be a short novella or a smaller size nonfiction book.

That got him on a writing path which quickly became an extra source of income.

His old belief that "you are not a good dad if you follow your passion," is no longer there. His new belief is this: "Thanks to my passion I can take better care of my family. Passion is perseverance. Passion is manhood."

And of course, as a kid he had been told that he would never make a dime from his writing. Then he was told that because of his corporate job, it would look unprofessional for him to become a writer. But it doesn't matter, because he is not writing for fame, but as a passion project which easily turns into extra income for him and his family. It also helps him relax and destress from his day job.

Think beyond yourself, your mission, your purpose. The work you are meant to be doing. Who did you allow to enter your mind and why?

Now, look at your vision, the one we created in the previous chapter. Are there any voices in your head that you feel are preventing you from taking action? Perhaps you fear it will be hard or that it will take too long, or that you will get laughed at.

What if there was a magical power that could totally erase those voices from your head? What if I told you there is a magic pill you can take, a pill you can use to erase self-doubt? Wouldn't that be helpful?

The good news is that pill exists, and it's called self-love. Do not allow other people's beliefs to become yours. Also, very often their

CHAPTER 4 ELIMINATE SELF-DOUBT

beliefs are not even their own in the first place. Once you start seeing how disempowered and easily influenced most people are, you quickly realize how necessary it is for you to transform so that you can set an example, shine your light and inspire others. Not by bragging and not by making them feel inferior. That stuff never works long term.

You can help other people by becoming the best version of yourself starting right here and now. You don't need to wait for the perfect moment. Be yourself and shine your light. Also, give yourself permission to follow your own pace. Remember, you don't fail - you succeed, or you learn.

Now, it's time for yet another awesome exercise...

Write down all the negative thoughts and everything you have been told you cannot do. Yes, I was told I should not be writing this book and that it was a waste of time. I was told many things that I decided to walk away from. And I am so happy I can finally be myself. I want to share it with other people.

Take a piece of paper and write down all your negative beliefs, negative self-talk and everything you think is a limiting belief. By now you should be able to spot them easily. If you still don't know how, here's the trick- if there is something you really want to do, and you think about it and you really feel light, but then you think about what you need to do to get there and you immediately start feeling heavy, it is a sign that there is some kind of a resistance showing up on your path. If the goal feels light, it is definitely for you. But then somewhere, somehow, you begin blocking your own way.

It's time for another emotional peeling!

On one piece of paper you will be writing down all the negative beliefs and opinions you realized are stopping you.

Then, start drawing hearts on them. Take a few deep breaths. Place your hands on your solar plexus.

CHAPTER 4 ELIMINATE SELF-DOUBT

Keep breathing. Say to yourself, I am ready to let go! I love you, I love me, I love me, and I love you.

You can also say, "Elena loves me".

Keep that piece of paper in front of you. Take another piece of paper and start rewriting negativity into positivity.

For example:

"Eating healthily is not for me, I can't eat this way, I don't like the taste."

Becomes:

"I have been watching some videos and reading eBooks about healthy recipes. The authors of that content all used to be overweight and unhealthy. But now they say they love eating healthily and can teach me how to do it as well. If they can do it, I can do it too. I can easily learn at least one new, healthy recipe a week. I can also learn healthy meal plans. There are many delicious recipes I can find and enjoy, and I can skip the recipes I don't like."

Be creative and repeat this process with all your limiting beliefs.

Once you have rewritten all the limiting beliefs into positive and empowering ones, allow yourself to destroy the first sheet of paper, where you write all the negative beliefs. While doing it say, "I love me, I love you. I love me I love you, I let go of you limiting beliefs, because you no longer serve me, but I am grateful for you because thanks to you, I was able to create my empowering beliefs instead."

And remember- Elena loves you! You are an amazing human being and you are here to follow your heart, your light and your passion. I am here to help you and guide you on your journey the best as I can.

Good stuff may take some time, but you're on your way. By aligning yourself with your actions, no matter how small they are, you are also aligning yourself with the infinite light of self-love. You are allowing yourself to take care of your body, mind and soul.

CHAPTER 4 ELIMINATE SELF-DOUBT

Self-love is very often depicted as self-care or doing some "girlish" stuff like getting your make-up or nails done.

But, in reality, self-care forms part of self-love. It's all interconnected. Taking care of your body helps you take care of your mind and soul. Taking care of your mind and soul helps you take care of your body.

Everything starts in your mind. Your precious mind. Own it, it's yours. Do not allow other people's opinions enter it, unless their opinions are helpful for you your journey.

Still, don't beat yourself up because there will always be some negative voices entering your mind. But now, you have the power. Now you know how to respect and love yourself enough to get rid of those limiting beliefs.

Stay strong and enjoy the cleansing benefits of re-writing your negative beliefs into the positive ones.

Chapter 5 Step #5 Expressing Kindness

Self-love and loving others are interconnected. By allowing yourself to be kind, in an authentic way, you can massively speed up the process of transforming your life.

I remember that when I first got started on the path of self-love, I was very excited because I had seen this huge power and potential, something that could really change my life on a deeper level. However, there were a few things that were holding me back.

1. Lack of patience
2. Relapsing back into negative patterns
3. Losing motivation

That's a "nice" mix, isn't it?

So, let me tell you what exactly was happening in my life back then and how you can protect yourself from those negative patterns.

Lack of patience, relapsing into old habits and losing motivation are all interconnected. Seems pretty obvious right? You get impatient, you get pulled back into old negative patterns and then you lose motivation. But the real issue is not lack of patience, relapsing into old patterns, and losing motivation. The real issue is how you deal with it and how those relapses make you feel.

The way most people react, and I used to be there too, is to feel guilty and develop some new negative beliefs on that foundation. You know, things like, "I can't stick to anything"; "Other people can do it"; "I lack discipline"; "Something is wrong with me".

No, nothing is wrong with you, in fact everything is fine. The above-mentioned reactions are normal and human. You will be pulled back into them many times, and so will I and so will be any spiritual gurus.

CHAPTER 5 EXPRESSING KINDNESS

Of course, they don't talk about it, because they are just perfect and everything what they say is perfect! That is the perfect world. But in the real world, things are different, and we live in the real world not in an ivory tower.

Our reactions are human and normal. Sometimes, our minds make us relapse a bit into negative patterns. One thing we can control is our reaction. The reason that we very often get pulled back into negative patterns of self-hate, self-guilt or addictions can be also because we don't allow ourselves to focus more on others.

And I am telling you- the best motivation is to think outside of yourself. And the best way to think outside of yourself is by performing random acts of kindness.

This is the concept I learned from an author, John Magee and his book, *Kindness Matters*.

Following the inspiration I got from his book, I quickly discovered that, by setting up a simple daily goal of for example:

-Sending out five genuine messages to people I am grateful for and appreciate

-Volunteering to help my local community

-Walking around and expressing my kindness as soon as I see something or someone I like. (Okay. That sounds weird, I know, I will elaborate more on that later.)

We are talking about authentic kindness not artificial kindness. You can walk away from things you don't like, it's fine. You are not a hater because of that. People have different tastes.

But...think of three or five people who inspire you. Message them and express your kindness and gratitude. It can be someone you know personally, or it can be someone you follow online, maybe a blogger or someone who shares their wisdom via videos.

CHAPTER 5 EXPRESSING KINDNESS

Message them or comment on their work and express your kindness. How does it feel?

Another way is to volunteer to help your local community. You will immediately start putting your focus and attention on other people and by doing that you will be stepping into love and light. By loving others, you love yourself and by loving yourself you love others.

For me, volunteering for my local community was an amazing experience. I also discovered some of my hidden gifts and met people who I truly believe were what I like to call "Manifestation Messengers". Those Messengers connected me to many amazing ideas and encouraged me to follow my passion in a meaningful and empowered way.

Had I not decided to volunteer back then, I wouldn't be where I am right now. Quite probably I wouldn't be even writing this book.

Another thing that you can immediately implement are random acts of kindness or compliments that you offer as you walk around your town. It can be something simple as offering someone a ride or helping them with their shopping. Or knocking on your old neighbors' door and asking if they need help around the house, or maybe if they want some fresh fruits and veggies.

At the same time, if you see someone wearing a nice dress or looking great in that new haircut, then tell them. Express your kindness and compliments: "Wow, I really like your new hair!"

Do it in an authentic way. It's not about forcing yourself to pay compliments to everyone. It's more about allowing yourself to express your positive thoughts with an intention of lighting everyone up.

The world needs more of those local, empowering leaders. Think about it. There are many people who wake up feeling miserable. They walk around feeling depressed and they go to bed feeling sad. Don't you think that they deserve an act of kindness? An authentic

CHAPTER 5 EXPRESSING KINDNESS

one. The one that will make them click. The one that will initiate their own journey of self-love.

The world doesn't need another "guru" from the ivory tower. The world needs us, small self-love leaders who are in the trenches, working on ourselves and living in the real world and overcoming real obstacles.

Now, it's your turn. Which act of kindness are you going to perform today?

Please let us and other people in our community know how this step worked out for you. Did you feel this instant vibrational shift? Didn't it feel good to be able to help someone, or even to make someone smile?

Share your experience related to random acts of kindness as well as your self-love journey and honest thoughts you have about this book so far, in the review section on Amazon. Your feedback can inspire and enlighten other readers on their journeys.

Finally, now that we have covered the importance and the healing power of random acts of kindness as well as thinking beyond yourself and helping people in your community, it's time to dive deeper into self-expression. This is one of the concepts very deeply connected with self-love.

Chapter 6 Step #6 Creative Self Expression

You are here for a reason. You are here to leave a legacy. You are here to inspire other people.

"Oh, Elena, but what if I don't want to be famous?"

Well, self-expression is much, much deeper and it doesn't have to be about becoming famous. Fame in itself is not bad at all. You can become famous in your field thanks to your work that is passion-driven and value-based.

It means that it consists exactly of those two components. You are passionate about what you do, and at the same time, you put that passion into creating value for other people.

Creative self-expression can be accomplished by social media or blogs. And, if you have that passion that driving force to help other people, something you have been wanting to share with the world for a while, don't wait to be perfect. Don't wait to be a perfect writer or speaker. Start now, start today, because you will get better and better as you go.

At the same time, creative self-expression can also be done through art, or even cooking. For example, if someone is passionate about smoothies, and they open their own smoothie bar- it's also creative self-expression.

The intention behind creative self-expression is always helping and inspiring other people while performing a meaningful action from a place of love and abundance.

Self-expression is deeply connected to self-love for multiple reasons.

One of them is that it helps rebalance our throat chakra in an authentic way. You see, if you have something valuable you know you need to be sharing, but you allow other people tell you what to do and what not to do and you suppress your wisdom, you are depriving your throat chakra of joy. Your ideas may very well disappear. The question is, will it be worth it?

For example, when I first got started on this writing journey, it was hard. I sometimes got hate emails or very rude reviews. I am not referring to honest feedback, where someone says, "Here is what I liked/ this could have been better/ I would have liked more information about…"

I am talking about nasty troll reviews. Like, "It's a scam that book only has one hundred pages." (The product information is there for you to check before you order. I could go to a vegan restaurant and complain that they don't do meat, or I could go to a steak house and complain they don't do vegan burgers.)

Those things happen. People who post those comments need self-love. To be honest, last year I took many months off writing and was going to quit at some point. My fear was, "What if it really takes off and I start getting more of those comments?"

I was feeling really upset. Finally, I reached out to a mentor who was a successful writer and she told me this:

"Really? Why do you think you should stop? Isn't it the trap of your own perception? Nasty negative comments show only one thing. Those people need more love and self-love. Those comments are just a reminder from the universe that the world needs you. What happened for you, happened for a reason. A person who leaves nasty comments very often comes from a dark place. Who knows what happened in their lives?".

"On the internet they feel safer and they can say whatever they want without showing their face. In real life they may be very shy people and they wouldn't even talk to you. Who knows what is really happening there?"

"At the same time, hate is not the answer. Love is the answer. Do you think it's really worth stopping? Think about your vision. Your

CHAPTER 6 CREATIVE SELF EXPRESSION

vision is to be writing every day and connecting with your readers. Your vision is to be getting emails from people whose lives were transformed thanks to your writing and what you share. What you have created so far is just a warm up. The signs you are getting from the Universe are amazing. Start by loving yourself more and then teach others by sharing your gifts and wisdom."

Wow, that gave me lots to think about and I decided to change my perception. Now, my question is- what about you? What is blocking you from expressing yourself?

Remember, you don't need to go public with it. Maybe you just want to take those dancing classes. That is also self-expression. Maybe, you want to learn a foreign language? Maybe you want to write children's book? Or perhaps you want to start a personal blog, just sharing your thoughts? How about drawing and doing your art? Or maybe learning to play the piano or guitar? Music is a very transformative power. It's therapeutic both for the creator and the receiver.

At the same time, maybe you feel you have many valuable thoughts you can share with other people? Well, start a new social media account where you can share and connect with like-minded individuals. Become a thought leader. As a thought leader, you can even write your own books, have a blog and start creating courses or retreats.

Traveling and exploring new places, as well as photography also form part of creative self-expression. Maybe you always wanted to be a travel blogger?

Whatever your choice is, the time is now. You know what it is. There is always something.

If you still struggle with finding your channel or form of self-expression, go back to your vision, the one we elaborated a few chapters ago. Ask yourself, "What does the new me do every day? What does the new me enjoy doing? What does the new me crave to be doing every day?"

CHAPTER 6 CREATIVE SELF EXPRESSION

Then, ask yourself, the new you from the future- and how did it all start? It started with one tiny decision, one tiny act of self-love. When I decided I am going to move forward. When I decided to love myself enough to get up and brush myself off and keep moving forward. It happened when I decided I would be a self-love warrior. That is when it happened.

Now, it's your turn. Think where you will be in the next five years. Feel it. And tune into that vision with your meaningful action. Your self-expression.

Chapter 7 Step #7 Positive Reminders and Your Own Magic Pendulum

It's time to have some fun! Your mind is stronger and much more powerful than you believe. And you already know you can actually control what you put in it. While there are many negative influences and opinions as well as detrimental messages out there, messages designed to get you off your self-love journey, you know your power. You know you're much stronger than that. You can easily design your own positive reminders and messages.

This is what we will be doing in this chapter, and yes, it does connect with the previous one, because we are embarking on creative self-expression again. So, just in case the last chapter felt like, "Okay, sounds great but I still don't know how to express myself", you can easily express yourself now.

All that can be easily amplifying your self-love.

So, let's do this! This process consists of three simple steps.

Step #1

Choose your place or places.

Ask yourself where you hang out most and what objects do you look at?

Think of your phone, your office, your computer, your book shelf, your fridge, your washing machine, dishwashing machine, your Kindle, your wardrobe, your bathroom.

We need to be very strategic here because the self-love reminders we will be planning will be very, very strong! While I am a big fan of small baby steps, in this case there will be no baby steps. We will be flooding the heck out of it!

CHAPTER 7 POSITIVE REMINDERS

So, write down all the places or objects you look at or happen to be at often or even multiple times of day.

Done, okay? Let's do the next step.

Step #2

Create a list of your favorite quotes and messages.

You can write down your own affirmations and thoughts or use quotes from people who inspire you.

One of my favorite quotes I like to use is by Tony Robbins, "The past does not equal to the future", or "It didn't happen to me, it happened for me."

Then, I also use a bunch of other reminders, such as, "I love you", "I love myself", "I love the person who I have chosen to become."

Now, it's your turn. Write it all down in your journal or on a piece of paper.

Step # 3

It's Shopping Time!

Whether from your local store or online, get some colored paper, stickers, or even beautiful postcards, and have fun with them.

Play your favorite music while you put your self-love messages and beautiful quotes on papers and stick them all around your house and other places you have chosen.

If you share your home with roommates or family members, you can either choose to put your self-love reminders only in your personal place like bathroom, or wardrobe or office, or you can choose to get them on the journey and go all in with self-love reminders and decorations.

As always, I am very curious to hear what you have come up with, so be sure to shoot me an email or post an Amazon review and let us know how this part of the process went and what you got out of the book and this particular chapter as well.

Many people simply reject this idea as childish. Or a waste of time. But thinking this way is very detrimental. We are always thinking. We think both consciously as well as subconsciously. The conscious thinking, for example, can be something like:

"Follow the to do list for today."

The subconscious thinking can be some kind of a trauma we decided to hide, because a few years ago someone told us something rude.

By choosing to use positive reminders we are inspiring our subconscious mind with tons and tons of positive messages. That creates the balance we need to step into the light, truth and alignment.

Choose to inspire and control your precious mind. Very often those reminders can save your day or turn a negative trigger into a positive thought and action. For example, in my kitchen I have lots of health self-love reminders, like "I love my body", "I choose to fuel my body", "I love who I am becoming", "I love health", "health is wealth", "health is life" and similar beautiful thoughts.

In my office I choose reminders like, "I am on my mission". "I am aligned to my purpose", "I write daily", "this is who I am". I also print out some emails I get from happy readers and look at them constantly because they definitely help me get rid of the writers' block.

Don't skip this step. Get creative here. I would even advise you to take a day off to do it. Combine it with some decluttering and cleaning if you want.

Chapter 8 #Step 8 Magnifying LOA Combine Action with Attraction

It's time to finish off with positive and inspired action. This handbook is not meant to be read and forgotten about. I want you to put the teachings into practice.

It's very important to track your self-love activities. Don't worry, we are not talking about some complicated rituals, or exercises that take lot of time. We have already done the hard part.

What I want to show you in this step is a very simple process I use daily to align myself with my vision and make sure I keep taking positive and inspired action.

You can transform this process to whatever you need to do or choose to do. You can create your own journaling practice as well. You can also choose to use one of my two branded journals.

You will find them at: LOAforSuccess.com/journals

Or by searching for them on Amazon (Search for: *Elena G. Rivers*).

That being said, in the morning, start off with writing down a few things you are deeply grateful for. It can be something related to your health, work or family. Whatever area of your life you want to focus on. You can even do a detailed gratitude ritual where you divide your gratitude journal or piece of paper into different columns or sections.

For example, health – what am I grateful for? You can list one or several things, depending on your time.

For example, I am grateful I am alive. I am grateful I can smile. I am grateful for all my senses.

You can even go deeper and be grateful for things you haven't received yet, but you know are coming. So, in the case of health,

CHAPTER 8 ACTION WITH ATTRACTION

wellness and fitness, perhaps you are giving yourself more self-love by eating a healthy, clean food diet? Maybe you start off your day with a little walk or workout?

And you know that by doing it every day, you will transform your body, or lose weight if that is your goal. That feels really amazing, because you know you are following a process that serves and you really trust that process.

On top of that, you are already grateful for the result you are looking to achieve but at the same time you are on the state of flow. And when you flow, you are free to eliminate resistance.

So, love yourself enough to be grateful even for things, results and circumstances that you still haven't received.

Like I said, you can focus on one area of your life that needs the most attention, or you can go ahead and write down a few pages where you express your gratitude for all areas of your life.

You can even switch it up depending on how you feel. Most people start off with just one area of their lives, the one that requires the most attention and self-love. The reason is that holistic success is all about creating balance. My balance may be different than yours because we have different goals, ambitions and preferences.

If you are feeling stuck in your life, chances are it's because of one area of your life that requires attention. The strong imbalance that manifests in one area of your life, very quickly will transfer to others causing havoc and imbalance.

So, love yourself enough to be honest with yourself and identify that one area of your life that requires the most attention from you, at the present time.

Whenever you have some free time, for example days off or weekends, you can allow yourself to journal and ground yourself for longer, simply by expressing gratitude for all areas of your life. Health, career, family, spiritual etc.

CHAPTER 8 ACTION WITH ATTRACTION

Now, the next step in the journaling process is to connect yourself with your vision for life, something that really excites you. Write down a few powerful and affirmative sentences that align you with that vision. There is no need to write a lot about it if you don't feel like it. Better to write a bit less, but really focus on your feelings and let go of all those negative voices in your head like, "I will never get there, I am not worthy, this is not for me."

No, no, no! You deserve all the good stuff. Self-love will get you there, trust me on that!

Close your eyes, breathe, you can listen to some music if you want.

Finally, it's time to plan your day. You already feel aligned to your vision, now ask yourself, "What kind of frequency do I need to get on today?" Again, don't force it. Just let it be. Some days might feel a bit less energetic, that's fine.

But you can still allow yourself to take meaningful and purposeful action to get closer to your vision. So, identify three simple mini actions to take today to give yourself the self-love you need to get closer to your vision. Embrace the here and now, the present moment where all the possibilities exist, right here and right now.

By starting off with gratitude, you get onto a higher vibration. Then, you connect with your vision and so you know where you're going. Now, ask yourself, "What can I do today? What kind of action, even imperfect, can I actually take today?"

Here's a simplified process that I have just explained in this chapter. Again, feel free to remodify it and turn it into a process that you will enjoy. It's something I recommend you do every morning (fifteen minutes should be enough). You can also do it in the evening, before you go to sleep, so that you plan ahead for the next day.

You can even go through the process twice a day if you really need it.

Step #1 Express deep gratitude, even for things you still haven't received but know are on their way. Really feel it.

CHAPTER 8 ACTION WITH ATTRACTION

Step #2 Align yourself with your vision by either writing it down, or meditating on it, really feeling, smelling or visualizing it.

Step #3 Plan out three simple mini actions for today, actions that are self-love based and can get you closer to your vision by helping you get to the new, more empowered you.

It's all about taking that meaningful, inspired action that comes from a sense of purpose, abundance and…yes you already know this – unconditional self-love, for your highest good and for the good of those around you.

Now, it's time for some self-love pleasure! The following pages contain the bonus content from Elena. The bonus full of amazingly healthy recipes as well as self-care rituals to help you take care of your mind, body and soul in a deeply nourishing way.

Bonus

Super Addictive Self-Love, Self-Care, Self-healing and Self-Wellness Recipes from Elena

Readers' transformation and inspirational results they can pass on to their loved ones are my biggest passion, mission and drive.

After writing my last book: "Law of Attraction to Make More Money"- even though success stories came quickly and the book helped many people, I also received some valuable feedback where a reader mentioned: "In your next book, can we get something simple to follow? Something we can do in our free time and something that becomes a process?"

That really got me thinking. Eventually, I got connected to an idea that really excited me. What if I could add some healing recipes? And rituals and self-healing formulas if you will.

The following bonus pages contain my best recipes that I use to align and treat my body and mind with love.

Then there is also a weekend plan you can do to fully recharge yourself. The weekend plan should be treated like a template. You can follow it if you wish, or you can follow yourself and use it as an inspiration.

I have even included my favorite plant-based recipes. I love pant-based food as it makes me feel really good and lighter. I just feel more energy which allows me to be more productive.

Whether you decide to eat that way all the time, or want to try it part time, I am sure you will find at least a few healthy healing recipes to add to your wellness routine.

BONUS: SELF-CARE RECIPES

Then, there is also a simple morning and evening ritual you can follow. The most important thing is to listen to your body. Give it what it needs but don't try to be perfect. Feel free to pick and choose.

BONUS: SELF-CARE RECIPES

Sweet Date Healing Smoothie

This is one smoothie that I turn to whenever I am craving sweets. The cinnamon in this smoothie helps to regulate blood sugar and insulin levels in the body. And it tastes so delicious you crave more and more of it.

Go for it, it's all guilt-free.

Serves: 1-2

Ingredients:
- 1/3 cup Medjool dates, pitted
- 1/2 cup ice
- 1 cup almond or any other nut milk of your choice
- ½ avocado (peeled and pitted)
- 1 teaspoon cinnamon powder
- Optional: 1 teaspoon melted coconut oil

Instructions:
1. Place all the above ingredients into the blender and mix/blend well.

BONUS: SELF-CARE RECIPES

Simple Cream Smoothie

This is an amazing smoothie recipe if you are craving something sweet and creamy.

Serves: 1
Ingredients:
- 1 avocado (peeled and pitted)
- 1 small banana, peeled
- 1 tablespoon chia seeds
- 1 teaspoon cinnamon powder
- 1 teaspoon cocoa
- 1 cup coconut milk

Instructions:
1. Blend all except the ice for as long as possible.
2. Pulse in ice or skip the ice and freeze for ½ hour.
3. Enjoy!

BONUS: SELF-CARE RECIPES

Mango Protein Smoothie

This smoothie is very high in protein and good fats which makes it an excellent breakfast smoothie as it will help you stay full till lunch.

Serves: 2
Ingredients:
- 1 frozen mango, chopped
- 3 tablespoons soaked almonds
- 1 tablespoon powdered chia seeds
- 1.5 cup almond milk
- 1 cup spinach
- Half an avocado, peeled, pitted
- Handful of blueberries

Instructions:
1. Blend all in a blender.
2. Enjoy!

BONUS: SELF-CARE RECIPES

Creamy Superfood Ice Cream

This creamy dessert is awesome for hot summer days. It's full of superfoods too. For example, maca powder helps rebalance hormones and Ashwagandha is an ancient Ayurvedic herb that helps sooth anxiety.

Serves: 1-2
Ingredients:
- 1 cup coconut milk
- Half cup fennel tea, cooled down
- 1 peach, peeled and pitted
- 1 banana, peeled
- Half teaspoon maca powder
- Half teaspoon Ashwagandha powder
- 1 inch piece fresh ginger, peeled
- 1 teaspoon lemon juice, fresh
- Some ice cubes

Instructions:
1. Place all the ingredients in a blender.
2. Blend until creamy and smooth.
3. Place in a freezer for a few hours.
4. Enjoy your healthy ice cream!

BONUS: SELF-CARE RECIPES

Sleep Well Tea

This recipe will help you unwind after a busy day, sleep like a baby and wake up feeling energized.

Serves: 2

Ingredients

- 1 cup water, boiling
- 1 lemongrass stalk
- 2 tablespoons chamomile tea
- A few tablespoons coconut milk
- 1 tablespoon coconut oil
- A dash of cinnamon powder to garnish

Instructions:
1. Place all the tea ingredients (except coconut milk and oil) in a tea pot and pour over some boiling water.
2. Keep covered for 15 minutes.
3. Strain.
4. Pour into a tea cup and add in the coconut milk and oil.
5. Stir well.
6. Sprinkle over some cinnamon powder, enjoy!

BONUS: SELF-CARE RECIPES

Easy Mediterranean Tea

I love this tea with my meditations!

Serves:2

Ingredients:

- 2 cups boiling water
- 1 tablespoon fresh rosemary herb
- 1 tablespoon fennel seeds
- 1 teaspoon green tea, or Melissa tea (optional)

Instructions:

1. Place all the tea ingredients (except honey) in a tea pot and pour over some boiling water.
2. Keep covered for 15 minutes
3. Strain and serve warm (but not boiling) in a tea cup with 1 teaspoon of honey (if needed)

BONUS: SELF-CARE RECIPES

Lime Refresher Iced Tea

Serves: 4-6

Ingredients

- 2 cups blueberries
- 2 limes
- 1 medium bunch of fresh oregano
- 1 liter filtered water

Instructions

1. Pour the water in to a suitable container or jug.
2. Wash the blueberries and limes.
3. Add the blueberries to the water, squashing a third of them on to a plate beforehand, and catching any juice to add too.
4. Juice one of the limes and add the juice to the water. Slice the other lime in to thin pieces.
5. Wash the oregano and give it a bit of a "squeeze" to start releasing some of its flavor.
6. Add the herbs to the water and mix really well. Leave in the fridge for at least an hour before serving.

BONUS: SELF-CARE RECIPES

Easy Sweet Potato Curry

This recipe is a real pleasure for your taste buds!

Serves: 2

Ingredients:

- 1 cup chickpeas, cooked and drained
- 2 tablespoons olive or coconut oil
- 4 medium sized sweet potatoes, peeled and cubed
- 1 onion, diced
- 1 tablespoon ginger powder
- 1 tablespoon curry powder
- ½ cup vegetable stock
- 1 can full fat coconut milk
- salt and pepper to taste

To garnish:

A handful of cilantro and mint leaves

Instructions:

1. Add 1 tablespoon olive or coconut oil to a skillet and heat up on medium-high heat.
2. Add the onions and cook until translucent.
3. Reduce to low/medium heat and add ginger, garlic and curry powder, and pinch of Himalayan salt cooking for another 2 minutes.
4. Now add the potatoes and vegetable stock. Keep stirring.
5. When almost soft, add chickpeas and coconut milk. Stir again. Turn off the heat when potatoes are done.
6. Garnish with cilantro and mint leaves. Enjoy!

BONUS: SELF-CARE RECIPES

Self-Love Panna Cotta

This recipe is one of my favorite guilt-free desserts.

Serves: 2-3

Ingredients:

- 1 cup coconut milk
- 1 cup almond milk (unsweetened)
- 2 tablespoons of unflavored gelatin
- 2 tablespoons stevia or honey
- 2 teaspoons vanilla extract
- 2 teaspoons cinnamon powder
- Juice of 1 lemon
- 2 tablespoons chia seeds
- Toppings of your choice (maybe homemade marmalade or some fruit?)

Instructions:

1. Pour the milk mix into a saucepan and add in gelatin.
2. Whisk steadily for 5 minutes (no heat).
3. Then, add in honey, cinnamon, vanilla, chia seeds and green powders (this is optional).
4. Turn on the heat (medium heat) and keep stirring constantly, until milk is hot enough to steam.
5. Important- Do not boil as this will deactivate the gelling properties of the gelatin.
6. Turn off the heat and leave to cool down for a few minutes.
7. In the meantime, grease small bowls with coconut oil and pour the heated mixture into the bowls.
8. Cover and place in the fridge for about 8 hours.
9. Serve and enjoy!

BONUS: SELF-CARE RECIPES

Cinnamon Quinoa Bowl

Servings: 2

Ingredients:

- 1 cup uncooked quinoa
- 1 ½ cups water
- ½ teaspoon ground cinnamon
- Pinch of Himalayan salt

Instructions:
1. Rinse the quinoa well.
2. In a medium-sized saucepan, combine the quinoa, water, cinnamon and salt.
3. Bring to a boil.
4. Then, turn down the heat, cover, and simmer for 10 minutes.
5. When cooked, remove from the heat.
6. Cool down.
7. Serve drizzled with coconut or almond milk.
8. Enjoy!

BONUS: SELF-CARE RECIPES

Sweet Dreams-Fight Insomnia Essential Oil Blend

(EO stands for Essential Oil)

Before using aromatherapy and essential oils, be sure to consult with your physician, especially if you're on medication, pregnant or suffering from any chronic diseases.

Blend:

- 2 tablespoons of coconut oil or olive oil (sesame oil works great too)
- 2 drops of verbena EO
- 2 drops of lavender (or lavandin) EO
- 2 drops of mandarin EO

Add to your Epsom salt bath or use for self-massage.

*An Epsom salt bath is a bath enriched with Epsom salt. You can easily purchase Epsom salt online. It's very inexpensive and extremely relaxing.

For Your Soul!

This holistic recipe will help you wake up and restore your energy levels. You can also use it for meditation, as it will help you keep centered.

Blend:

- 1 tablespoon of coconut oil
- 2 drops of citronella EO
- 1 drop of cinnamon EO
- 1 drops of bergamot EO

- 1 drop of ylang ylang

Add to your Epsom salt bath or use for self-massage.

Massage instructions:

1. Massage your neck, chest, and shoulders. Head massage with oils can be extremely energizing too.
2. You will find the balance between citric scents like citronella and bergamot spiced up by floral ylang ylang fragrance and cinnamon mystery.
3. Bergamot is also a great anti-anxiety remedy as my next recipe explains.
4. Remember- no sunbathing after this massage! Citric oils are photo-toxic.

No More Anxiety!

If you feel like anxiety is knocking on your door, make sure you take a few deep breaths and confide in aromatherapy and Epsom salt combo.

With this blend you can take a holistic approach and get to the root of the problem.

This is so much better than standard anti-anxiety pills that only make us sick and tired (and very often fat).

An Epsom salt bath is a great source of magnesium (a mineral you need to fight stress). If you combine it with essential oils, you will give yourself an amazing mix of all-natural ingredients to fight anxiety.

BONUS: SELF-CARE RECIPES

Blend:

- 2 tablespoons of coconut oil
- 2 drops of bergamot EO
- 2 drops of verbena EO
- 2 drops of basil EO (refrain from using this oil if you are suffering from clinical depression).

Add to your Epsom salt bath or use for self-massage.

Massage Instructions:

- You can do a full body massage.
- Concentrate on your feet and solar plexus.
- Breathe in and out in a conscious way.

BONUS: SELF-CARE RECIPES

Bonus: How to Practice Mindfulness Meditation

Practicing mindfulness meditation is quite simple and does not require a lot of preparation or training. Anyone can get into it. All you have to do is make a little time. *Learning how* to do the practice *is* the practice.

To begin with, set aside five to ten minutes of your day, every day. Find a quiet place to sit- a nice warm bath is great for that. Whatever works for you.

Your eyes can be open or closed; it's up to you. You may find that closing your eyes helps keep you from distraction, at least in the beginning.

The basic practice of sitting meditation is just to place your mind on the breath. *Mindfulness* in this context means being mindful of the breath, just following it as it moves in and out. When thoughts and sensations arise, you notice them and simply return your attention to the breath. It does not really matter what kind of thoughts or feelings come up. They could be boring thoughts about what you need to get from the store, or they could be mean, angry, happy, funny, creative, passionate—whatever.

Whatever comes up, just mentally label it *thinking* and return your attention to the breath. That's the nonjudgmental awareness we talked about earlier—whatever comes up, don't try to decide whether it's good or bad, don't accept or reject it. Just gently say to yourself, *thinking*, and gently redirect your attention to the breath.

As you follow the breath in and out, you want to pay attention to the sensation of the breath—the feeling of the cool in-breath on your nostrils, and the warmth of the out-breath, the rise and fall of your lungs as you breathe in and out, whether the breath is long or short, shallow or deep, hard or gentle, and so on. In general, when meditating on the breath, you don't try to change the quality of the breath, but just let your lungs breathe however is most natural at any given time and watch that.

Breathing is an effortless, autonomic function of the body, so we normally don't pay any attention to it. It just goes on in the background, all the time. In the practice of mindfulness, however, we don't take the breath for granted. Instead, we learn to appreciate the breath in its simplicity and variation. We develop a sense of wonder at something so simple and so necessary—taking in lungfuls of healthful, life-giving oxygen, which are delivered to the different organs of our body by the circulation of our blood. If we can learn to love and appreciate the simple fact of being alive, we can love ourselves.

When you begin meditating, it may seem that your discursive thoughts, the so-called "monkey mind," have only increased. Actually, nothing has increased; you just never normally noticed how active your mind is. Just stick with the practice of remaining mindful of the breath. Slowly, the speed of your thoughts will decrease. You will begin to notice and enjoy the vivid richness of the direct, sensory quality of your experience. This is the beginning of coming in touch with a quality of yourself that is fundamentally awake. It is the discovery of an innate source of goodness deep within your being.

Making friends with yourself

By bringing your awareness to the breath and learning to appreciate the simplicity of the present moment, you develop a sense of love for yourself that is not based on stories that you tell yourself, your wishes, likes and dislikes, who you tell yourself you want to be, negative thoughts, and so on. Instead, this newfound self-love is based on a direct, honest relationship to your own mind. This relationship is what has been called *making friends with yourself*.

The very act of meditation is an act of kindness to yourself. By setting aside time to rest and watch the breath, you are demonstrating a willingness and a commitment to sit with yourself quietly and gently. That is an act of compassion, a declaration of unconditional friendship to yourself and a willingness to get to know your own mind and heart more deeply.

It may sound strange to hear, but most of us do not really know ourselves that well. That's because we never take the time to get to know ourselves. So, it's important to take that time, to slow down and rest. In this state of rest, we become more familiar with our own thoughts and feelings. Through the process of making friends with ourselves in meditation, we equip ourselves with self-love and self-compassion. Thus, we can forgive ourselves when we make mistakes, or offer ourselves gentle encouragement and advice when we feel overwhelmed or anxious. This becomes a safeguard against the pessimism that attacks our motivation.

BONUS: SELF-CARE RECIPES

Your Simple Self-Love Plan for the Weekend or a Day Off

Saturday, or Sunday (or both)

7:00 – Wake up, start focusing on things you are grateful for as you get up, drink water, brush your teeth, have a shower etc.

7:30 – 8:00 Meditation (can be also replaced by a walk, yoga or exercise)

8:00 -8:30 Healthy breakfast of your choice or a big smoothie

8:30- 9:00 Coffee, or tea and journaling

9:00 – 12:00 Get out in nature, walk, smile and enjoy the freshness, read or listen to something positive, jot down things in your journal.

12:00 – 13:00 – Healthy lunch, for example a salad and a big veggie smoothie

13:00- 14:00 – Little power nap while listening to a guided meditation

14:00 – 16:00 – Be out again. Walk, or cycle or just hang out in the park while spreading random acts of kindness.

16:00- 17:00 – Still out or back at home, use the inspiration you got from spreading the random acts of kindness to create more positive reminders, as described in the previous chapters. You can just write it all down in your journal and spread the reminders across your home and office later.

18:00- 19:00 Relaxing, Epsom salts bath combined with drinking herbal teas and smoothies.

19:00 – Out with people you love +dinner together, or, if needed spending time in solitude, reading a book or going through a course you enjoy and cooking a healthy dinner. For example, plant-based

Indian curry full of delicious spices (you can try my sweet potato curry I listed with my healing self-love smoothie recipes).

21:00 Meditation and evening ritual before going to sleep.

22:00 Listening to meditation of your choice before going to sleep. Visualize and tune into your desired reality. It's already happening.

BONUS: SELF-CARE RECIPES

Bonus – Empowering Self-Love Morning and Evening Ritual

Morning Ritual

Step #1 Drink clean, filtered water with lemon.

Step #2 Walk, jog, dance, or do yoga. Even five minutes is enough to raise your vibration. Listen to your favorite music.

Step #3 Have a shower. Massage your body. You can use coconut oil with a few drops of a soothing lavender oil.

Step #4 Meditate and journal

Step #5 Have a healthy breakfast or a power smoothie.

The smoothie I like to make in the morning is:

1 small banana + 1 small avocado + 1 orange + 1 cup coconut milk + half teaspoon cinnamon + ¼ teaspoon maca powder + ¼ teaspoon Ashwagandha + 1 tablespoon chia seeds.

I blend the smoothie, put it in a smoothie bowl and throw in some almonds. Sometimes I add in cocoa powder or cocoa ribs.

That smoothie is great for breakfast, tastes really nice, is sweet, has food fats and natural protein and helps me stay energized for hours.

It makes my belly happy and I don't feel like craving processed foods. I just enjoy the natural sweetness of this smoothie.

Try it!

Step #6 Read a few pages of a book (or listen to something positive, it can be a podcast or an audiobook you listen to on your way to work. In case you're wondering- yes, all my books are also available as audiobooks for this purpose, so if you feel like it, you can feed your mind with positive information even if you are too busy to read).

Step #7 Stand in front of the mirror and congratulate yourself on completing your morning ritual. Now you are ready to really smash it! You are aligned and energized and ready to go.

Note: Some days you will not be able to go through all the steps, and that is totally fine. Just pick one thing. Or set up a timer and meditate for five minutes.

Small actions are better than no actions. Also, even if you do something super small, super micro, for example you meditate for only one minute, remember that you still deserve to reward yourself because you are moving forward and that deserves to be celebrated.

Evening Ritual

Step #1 Have a nice, nourishing dinner and if needed, make a smoothie for the next morning, or prepare some healthy food.

(While preparing your food, talk to a loved one by calling them or listen to some positive podcast or audiobook.)

Step #2 Enjoy a nice, relaxing bath with essential oils and Epsom salt. Use incense and candles if needed and play some relaxing music. Sip on healing, herbal infusions.

Step #3 Meditate

Step #4 Journal or read through what you have written in your journal so far. Tracking our thoughts and progress is very therapeutic. If you need more journaling guidance, I also offer two branded journals: *Gratitude AMPLIFIER Journal* as well as *Law of Attraction for Abundance Journal (you will find them at: LOAforSuccess.com/journals)*

Step #5 Allow yourself to fall into well-deserved sleep to rest your beautiful body, mind and soul. Listen to some relaxing music or

BONUS: SELF-CARE RECIPES

guided meditations if needed. Ask yourself what you need most. Music? Silence? Meditation?

For me, I love listening to recordings of nature sounds, like seagull, sound waves. My dream is to be living in a house on the beach, and write from there, every day while overlooking the ocean. By listening to the sound of ocean I align myself with my vision. I also play similar recordings while writing and I feel as if it was happening right now.

What about you? What is your vision? What do you want to feel aligned to?

Let me know by emailing me or leaving me an honest review on Amazon.

I am also curious to see if you enjoyed the bonus recipes and are planning to use them.

MORE BOOKS BY ELENA

A Special Offer from Elena to Help You Manifest Faster

Finally, I would like to invite you to join my private mailing list (my **VIP LOA Newsletter**). Whenever I release a new book, you will be able to get it at a discounted price (or sometimes even for free, but don't tell anyone 😊).

In the meantime, I will keep you entertained with a free copy of my exclusive LOA workbook that will be emailed to you when you sign up.

To join visit the link below now:

www.loaforsuccess.com/newsletter

After you have signed up, you will get free instant access to this exclusive workbook (+ many other helpful resources that I will be sending you on a regular basis).

If you have any questions, please email us at: support@loaforsuccess.com

MORE BOOKS BY ELENA

More Books written by Elena G. Rivers

Available at: www.loaforsuccess.com

Ebook – Paperback – Audiobook Editions Available Now

Law of Attraction for Amazing Relationships

Law of Attraction for Weight Loss

MORE BOOKS BY ELENA

Law of Attraction for Abundance

Law of Attraction Manifestation Exercises

You will find more at:

www.loaforsuccess.com/books

MORE BOOKS BY ELENA

www.ingramcontent.com/pod-product-compliance
Lightning Source LLC
Chambersburg PA
CBHW071007080526
44587CB00015B/2371